FOURTH LEADERS

Printed in Great Britain

FOURTH LEADERS

FROM

THE TIMES

1950

*A selection
from the past
twelve months*

LONDON

THE TIMES PUBLISHING COMPANY LIMITED
PRINTING HOUSE SQUARE

INTRODUCTION

THIS COLLECTION OF essays is the second of a series. The first, which appeared last year, was welcomed by the public, the entire edition being sold out in a very short space of time. Like its predecessor's, the contents of *Fourth Leaders from The Times*, 1950, have been selected from the light leaders which have been published during the last twelve months ; and, like its predecessor, it will be followed by a similar volume about this time next year, for it is intended that the appearance of these harmless and perhaps even edifying volumes will be an annual event.

For how long this intention will continue to be carried out is, of course, a matter for speculation. Will there ever be such a book as *Fourth Leaders from The Times*, 2050 ? Some would argue that this is improbable. By that date, they will contend, either chaos or Utopia will reign in these islands, and the British of the period will be either too brutalized or too enlightened to have any time for Fourth Leaders.

But even Utopia, one suspects, will have its funny side ; and we have all been near enough to chaos to doubt whether its worst terrors can altogether extinguish laughter. So it seems just possible that a series whose sole and unpretentious aim is to amuse may have a longer life than more important and ambitious enterprises ; and here, at any rate, is the second volume in it.

CONTENTS

ON TRYING TO BE FUNNY

There are few of us who have not, at some stage of our career, been accused of trying to be funny. Sometimes the charge was a just one ; we were indeed deploying our slender wit or our possibly rather abstruse sense of humour in an attempt to amuse. At other times it was not true that we were trying to be funny ; we were merely doing or saying something of a nature which seemed to our accuser disconcerting and incomprehensible. In either case there was always a peculiarly tart, an almost venomous, note in the accusation. To try to be funny, it was forcefully implied, was a peculiarly despicable thing to do. It was not merely that the words, and the manner in which they were spoken, made it quite clear that our attempt at humour was a humiliating failure. It was worse than that. The mere making of the attempt, we were given sharply to understand, was in some un-explained way heinous and anti-social.

" He's always trying to be funny "—how painful an image the words conjure up, how firmly we shun the society of the person to whom they are applied. Yet no one is taken to task for trying to be gloomy (a far easier assignment) ; and people who make this endeavour, in which the risks of failure are for most of us minimal, often earn the approbation of their fellows and the repu-tation of being fearless realists. It seems somehow to be assumed that funny people can and ought to be funny without making the slightest effort ; it is the fact of trying that attracts to itself so much ridicule and contempt. Perhaps the humorists, the comedians, and the clowns are at fault for making it all seem so easy. Perhaps those who seek, in however humble a sphere, to emulate them deserve to be checked for their presumption. Yet it does

1

A

seem slightly unfair that anyone who does his poor best to increase the nation's stock of gaiety should lay himself open to a damaging accusation, whereas those who try to reduce it by their mournful and alarming predictions run no comparable risk. We cannot all be funny, though the world would probably be a pleasanter place if we were; but it is difficult to see where the harm lies in trying to be so, as long as our experiments are conducted in a humane and genteel manner. They had better be successful, too.

STREET NAMES

On her recent visit to Exeter PRINCESS ELIZABETH inaugurated the rebuilding of the bombed parts of the city by naming a new street Princesshay. This was a pleasant inspiration, not only because it will permanently recall a happy occasion in Exeter's history, but because the new name conforms with the two time-honoured ones of its main thoroughfares, Northernhay and Southernhay. It is not all city fathers that have so felicitous a model ready to their hands, and the naming of new streets must often present a difficult problem. Even as the postman probably, and the inquiring visitor certainly, prefers a row of numbered houses to " Chez Nous " and " Glenside," so there is much to be said for some such system as that of the New York streets, combining numbers with points of the compass. It is a great help to the stranger striving to find his way, but it is a plan lacking something of romance and so disappointing to those who love names for their own sake. It is again a regrettable fact that street names making the strongest appeal to the sightseer may not be so agreeable to the inhabitants, especially those who earn their living there. There is, if memory serves, a Quiet Street in Bath and a Silent Street in Ipswich. Here are two enchanting names which " impart to the relieved pedestrian the sensation of having put cotton in his ears and velvet soles on his boots " ; but they might conceivably be deemed bad for business. A man could dwell happily for ever in Crooked Usage, but he might think twice before setting up his shop there.

Yet this is a view that may easily be exaggerated and sometimes the inhabitants have a greater love for what is old and romantic and so far better sense than the local authorities. On the outskirts of a great western city

3

there is a road called Plunder Street, recalling the time when highwaymen lay in wait there for coaches. It was proposed, doubtless with the best intentions, to change the name to one of a deadly and decent dullness, whereupon there was a levy *en masse* of the neighbourhood to protest against the outrage and Plunder Street gloriously remains. There is often much useful knowledge to be learnt from street names. Major Pendennis, who begged his nephew to read Debrett daily in order to avoid social solecisms, must often have felt his breast swell as he contemplated the streets and squares of London, so full of instruction are their names as to the seats and subsidiary titles of noble families. Changes there must be and the cluster of streets which once, we are told, commemorated at full length CHARLES VILLIERS, DUKE OF BUCKINGHAM, is not quite what it was ; but if " Of Alley " has long departed, Villiers Street and Buckingham Street are still there. Much humbler and more local history is often to be traced. There must be numberless villages in England which still have a Mill Lane. The mill is gone but the sound of its sails still agreeably haunts the lane. District councils ought to deal very tenderly with these ancient names and if they want new ones an old map will often provide something far better than their own prosaic and lamentable inventions.

THE OLD SHOT TOWER

Londoners, who rarely pass a building under construction and even more rarely stop to look at one when it is completed, have at present an unrivalled opportunity to indulge their passion for chaos in its most primitive form in the half-dozen acres of mud and machinery that lie between the south bank of the Thames and Belvedere Road. It is here that the topless towers of the Festival of Britain will rise in 1951, if they are not lopped in half by MR. ATTLEE's little axe, and it is here that the concrete pillars of the new Concert Hall may already be seen groping their way out of the mud rather like MR. ORSON WELLES's fingers emerging from the sewers of Vienna in that admirable film, *The Third Man.* To the true connoisseur, however, it is not the vision of the future that matters, nor even the splendid view of the north bank that has been revealed ; it is the matchless confusion which seems to reign there and now. At one point earth's foundations quiver under the blows of a monstrous steam hammer ; at another giant machines scoop earth out of one hole in order to deposit it in another. Everywhere pumps suck and gurgle as they pour water—if such it can be called—back into the Thames,

> than whom no sluice of mud
> With deeper sable blots the silver flood.

Half an hour can pass delightfully in simply watching the hoses as they pant and palpitate like a frog in the hand.

In all this scene of animated desolation only two objects —if we except Hungerford Bridge itself—stand apart, solid, immobile, and reasonably complete. They are the old Shot Tower and the wych-elm which droops disconsolately beside it. The wych-elm, carefully fenced in

5

lest the careless driver of a scoop should snatch it up by the roots, is a pleasant reminder that nature will return one day even if expelled by a bull-dozer. Seeing it, one can imagine—with a little effort—other trees planted by MR. MORRISON with a silver trowel and even velvet lawns stretching to the river as they do in the illustrated brochures. The Shot Tower, on the other hand, is a more disturbing symbol. It is, after all, a work of man if not a work of art, and it is bound to raise some awkward questions.

Once before the Shot Tower played a brief part in an aesthetic controversy. In 1821, to be precise, the REVEREND W. L. BOWLES dragged it into his " Strictures on the Life and Writings of Pope." " What," wrote the REVEREND BOWLES, " makes the venerable towers of Westminster Abbey more poetical, as objects, than the tower for the manufactory of patent shot, surrounded by the same scenery ? " BYRON, to whom a copy had been sent in Italy, replied in a long, indignant letter to JOHN MURRAY. The answer, he said—very justly—was " architecture," and added :

Ask a foreigner on his approach to London what strikes him as the most poetical of the towers before him : he will point out Saint Paul's and Westminster Abbey, without, perhaps, knowing the names or associations of either, and pass over the tower for patent shot—not that, for anything he knows to the contrary, it might not be the mausoleum of a monarch, or a Waterloo column, or a Trafalgar monument, but because its architecture is obviously inferior.

It would be pleasant to think that foreigners approaching London in 1951 for the Festival of Britain will see new towers, more " poetical " and more beautiful than any at present visible, at least on the south bank. Perhaps they will. Yet such is our lack of confidence ever since the genius of architecture left us round about 1830 that no one can be quite sure. So the old Shot Tower remains, a little grim and clumsy, " functional " if ever a building deserved the name, looking like a lighthouse deserted by the sea, yet still a reminder of an age when

6

Englishmen did not know how to build badly. And from its summit visitors will be able to see, etched against the superb skyline from Westminster to St. Paul's, the domes and spires of a still greater age rising above the wreckage of the nineteenth and twentieth centuries.

WANTED—A MOUSE TRAP

Inventors like doctors have their Achilles heel. What the common cold is to a doctor, the mouse trap is to an inventor. Ask him to make an aircraft that lets you breakfast in China and lunch in Peru and, smiling tolerantly, he prepares to do the trick. Tell him that these autumn nights have brought their usual invasion of mice and the most he can as a rule do for you is to catch your fingers in an iron grip. Mice are the cause of acute attacks of split personality in the animal lover. Bright eyes, soft elegant fur and swift, graceful movement make them endearing little creatures, but they eat so much and make so horrid a mess of what they do not eat that there is nothing for it except to destroy them. Faced with his painful necessity, the agent of destruction seeks a humane and a fool-proof weapon and he is generally fobbed off with one that might, for all its claim to the second of these adjectives, have been invented by a working party of mice.

Gingerly he pushes back the guillotine part of the contraption after having baited the spike with an ill-spared morsel of his cheese ration. He is, when he begins this operation, already flustered, for self-styled experts have warned him that, if he squeezes the cheese on firmly with his hands the suspicious mice will reject it as being tainted by human scent, while, if he uses kid glove methods, it will be wedged too loosely and removed too safely. Having guided the straight bit of metal through the eye that holds up what may be called the drop he—with infinite caution—lets go. There is a terrifying snap, the whole box of tricks bounds on the kitchen table and all is to do over again. Nerves being now defeatist, the next attempt has for objective less the setting of a lethal trap

8

than the making certain that, as hands are removed, there will be no repetition of that noisy, premature discharge. The hook holds, the drop cants upward ready to fall beneath the weight of its victim and, sadly bowing to domestic necessity, the executioner, again proceeding with delicate circumspection, carries his loaded gadget into the larder and brings it softly to rest on a shelf where, overnight, mice had supped and gambolled.

Next morning the cheese is gone and so are the mice. Empty and unsprung, the trap is removed for testing and now proves so well and truly jammed that the most elephantine mouse, too sleek with the plunder of house-keeping to avoid getting wedged in the mouth of its hole, might, without fear of the consequences, dance a ballet on the death platform. A determined—an irritable —bang having set the thing reluctantly off, the baffled hunter finds himself back where he came in. Attempts to achieve a hair-trigger deftness imperil his fingers, while stability is only reached at the expense of the slightest chance of catching a mouse. This is humiliating for the large army of clumsy citizens and is made worse by the existence of a more nimble minority. To be nearly nipped and then made a fool of by some contemptuous spectator is a fate that, however salutary it may be to the proud spirit, should be prevented by the skill and cunning of inventors. Even the cat must some-times laugh as, curled up before the kitchen fire, it watches these abortive manoeuvres, although, if the truth be told, so many cats are such lazy mousers that straight faces would better become them.

HALF-TERM

School children, like convicts, serve sentences varying in length and in severity. Some are given ticket of leave every day to come home for tea to dictate which programmes shall be let loose on the wireless and, as they approach years of discretion, furtively to smoke their parents' cigarettes. Others are in for life, as it is measured by juvenile standards of time. Their bathing things or, for those who prefer the term, swim-suits, are scarcely dry from the last dip of the summer holidays when the prison gates close until Christmas. A middle party is enlarged at week-ends, or at some of them, between September and December, and members of it have just been open to grown-up inspection, as, indeed, have the life sentencers, who may be visited in captivity at half-term. Little or no anguish mars these fugitive reunions between parent and child. On the contrary, fathers and mothers, talking it over afterwards, agree that the school is evidently very nice, the masters and mistresses sympathetic without being weak and the pupils happy and burgeoning hopefully and not too quickly.

This complacence flourishes against a self-conscious background of how much worse matters were ordered in the past. Mr. Bultitude and his contemporaries are said to have asked for it with their cant about schooldays being the happiest times of our lives. All that bullying and bad food, the learning by heart, the washing in ice-cold water, the senseless—and so bad for hand-writing—copying of endless lines were blots on Mr. Bultitude's scutcheon. He deserved everything he got when the just magic of " Vice Versa " caught him in its toils. SIR MAX BEERBOHM, openly confessing that a glimpse of a victim being carted off to school filled him with pleasure at having

10

escaped the horrors of dormitory and classroom, was at least honest. Thank goodness our children are spared those old sufferings. Warmed by this sense of their own enlightenment, parents are given to wishing that they could have their time over again under the new order and to reviving memories of what, even in their comparatively recent days, they went through. Mothers recall the severity, unheard of by modern standards, of a head mistress and the ingenuity of a cook in evolving every Monday the same uneatable pudding. Fathers remember or invent cautionary tales of how they armoured themselves with brown paper against the scientific assaults of old So-and-So. The agreeable conclusion is thus reached that all is going well this term and that the older generation triumphantly survived ordeals to which the younger is not exposed.

Most of this may be true, but there is one catch in it that deserves notice. How many parents, having considered their children's working timetable, can honestly claim that they could stand the pace? From early morning until early bed, the focus shifts at short intervals from subject to subject. French grammar, Latin prose, the detective properties of litmus paper, the sources of *The Merchant of Venice*, the square on the hypotenuse of a right-angled triangle—all these in less than the course of one revolving moon clamour for attention. A day of it would drive the average adult mad. Even the miscellaneous demands of a single night's " prep " would send him reeling upstairs. The crowning mercy of being grown up is that it brings release from so many subjects hated at first sight but keeping themselves relentlessly in view through years of school. If children may no longer be pitied let them at least be saluted respectfully for the amazing versatility with which they submit to healthy hard labour.

11

DREAM TENANT

" Would suit diplomat." The words appear fairly regularly in advertisements offering vacant possession of houses or flats, and it is easy to see why. Suave, wealthy, discreet, the diplomat makes a far stronger *prima facie* appeal as a prospective tenant than the all-in wrestler, the ichthyologist, or the young couple with four adorable children and a bull-terrier. House-trained to a fault, he will in addition confer upon one's property a certain glamour and distinction ; and as we wait for him to answer our advertisement (on paper heavily embossed with the arms of Ruritania) it is a real pleasure to visualize him in residence. See him leave, as upon most evenings he undoubtedly will, to attend some glittering *soirée*. Immaculately cloaked and gloved, the Order of the Ocelot glittering darkly on his breast, he saunters down the front-door steps and, uttering some incomprehensible admonition to the driver, is whirled away in a huge black car of American manufacture. How different from our own exits—the cans of hot water poured into the bonnet of the gelid car, the petulant and unavailing whine of the self-starter, at last the departure, vaporous, convulsive, and twenty minutes late. The neighbourhood, we feel, will be all the better for a little *panache*.

Here, at our desk, he will sit, surrounded by photographs of grand duchesses and prime ministers in silver frames, thoughtfully penning his dispatches : reporting on the latest *démarche*, deflating *ballons d'essai*, poohpoohing the possibility of a *détente*, anatomizing the economies of SIR CRIPPS. From time to time he will entertain. Exotic fur coats will range themselves upon the counterpane in the spare bedroom, footmen will glide noiselessly to and fro proffering champagne, and

12

his guests (unlike ours) will be far too well bred to dream of putting their cigarette ends elsewhere than in the ashtrays.

It goes, somehow, without saying that he will be a diplomat of the old school, and not a representative of the whimsically self-styled New Democracies. Our house would suit them too, but would they suit it? We cannot feel certain on this point. We do not altogether like the idea of our dining room being the scene of toasts to the cause of world revolution. Still, we grow less particular as the days go by and no Excellency answers our advertisement. We visualize the Diplomatic Corps as being to a man childless, dogless, affluent, and, when they find out about the bathroom window, able to get it put right; and if a diplomat from beyond the Iron Curtain were to come along we should not allow ideology to interfere with our negotiations. If he wishes to indulge in clandestine activities, we shall point out, there is always the tool-shed.

BED-SITTERS

A distinguished periodical recently offered its sympathy to those unfortunate displaced persons—the inhabitants of bed-sitting rooms. That they are a growing community can be inferred from their *cris de coeurs* in the personal columns of *The Times*, but about their true predicament there is widespread unconcern. Bed-sitting rooms, unfortunately for their inhabitants, lack the necessary news value to catch the conscience of the world. They cannot compete for squalor with the dosshouse of GORKI or the workhouse of DICKENS, for colour with the old-world abandon of HOGARTH'S Gin Alley; and, although in this democratic age they are more deserving of our sympathy than the sceptred gloom of Elsinore or Cawdor, they lack the glamour of those royal enclosures.

There is, however, a new consideration which promotes the bed-sitting room into a major official problem. According to the statisticians quite a large number of Britain's Civil servants of all ages proceed each morning to their seats of power from the incongruous background of four heavily papered bed-sitting room walls. This is indeed a fact of consequence, the first ebb in the tide of resentment against officialdom, for however uncooperative Mr. Smith of the Ministry of Pensions may be in the day, the knowledge that his evenings are spent in a bed-sitting room should melt our hearts. Apart from sympathy, it is plainly to our disadvantage that he should pass in surroundings so uninspiring those hours at the end of the day that should be given to enjoyment. Nor is the manner of his getting up in the morning likely to encourage an understanding mood. The occupant of the bed-sitter is denied the early morning

14

indulgence that is indispensable—he can never scramble into his clothes after oversleeping, upturn his chest of drawers in the search for the right tie, and then descend to breakfast without a twinge of conscience, as if the very act of shutting the bed-room door would set the room to rights. The bed-sitter must eat his breakfast on the battlefield.

But what really makes the bed-sitting room so unsuitable an environment for the public servant is not the difficulty of eating, sleeping, shaving, reading, writing, and experiencing the myriad subtleties of being alive—all within four walls. Far more dangerous is the bed-sitting room's capacity for interfering at every point with the claims of what the Americans know as the gracious life. Take, for example, the field of romance. Courting is still a competitive undertaking and in its successful execution the bed-sitter carries a heavy handicap. His heart melting with adoration for some haughty beauty, he cannot evoke the twin genii of the kitchen and the cellar to aid him in his pursuit. Not for him that intimate flicker of candlelight on a table laid for two. Is it really possible to entertain with any degree of elegance in a room that contains one's pyjamas and one's butter ration, one's hair oil and one's Empire sherry, and in any case is there any reason to suppose that any well-brought-up young lady would feel herself at liberty to visit a gentleman's bed room just because it contained, in addition to the bed, an armchair and a toasting fork ?

Some may reply that a life without philandering, spent in vigorous masculine society, is admirably suitable for the aspiring public servant. But in the bed-sitting room even bachelor conviviality is barred. For those courageous bed-sitter hosts undeterred by the presence of only one chair there is always the danger of a complaint of disturbance from the lodger next door. Entertaining in such circumstances is undeniably risky. No, it is best to be realistic. Life in a bed-sitting room might have suited DIOGENES, did suit OBLOMOV, and would, no

15

doubt, suit GRETA GARBO if fate had not willed it otherwise ; but for Civil servants, on whose companiable instincts and cheerful disposition we are all so intimately dependent, the bed-sitting room is quite the wrong accommodation.

CONSEQUENCES OF A SNEEZE

Some of us are bigger moral cowards than others, but we are all tainted with this failing. One of its commonest manifestations is a tendency to write off personal possessions whose recovery would make us conspicuous and would inconvenience other people. The sixpence which, dropped at the window of the booking office, scurries off among the legs of the queue like a hare dodging through kale; the library book which, as a glacier of humanity carries us out of the cinema at the end of the last performance, we remember to have left in the two-and-ninepennies; the packet of sandwiches unaccountably extruded from our pocket as the field moves off towards the covertside—these losses most of us do nothing to retrieve. We suppress them. We even sometimes pretend not to have noticed them, and when some friendly horseman, pointing to the small white object among the trampling hooves, informs us that we have dropped our sandwiches, we simulate surprise. " Oh, have I? " we say, " Never mind. I've got more than I want anyhow " we add, lapsing into a deliberate untruth. And we urge our horse forward, away from the scene of a crime against our conscience.

Of what far nobler, sterner stuff is constructed the character of the Canadian engine-driver who, as our Ottawa Correspondent reports, lost his false teeth over-board while engaged in the performance of his duties! A sneeze caused these valuable appendages to leap from his jaws and bite the dust of the so extensive prairie, and their owner hurtled onwards, toothless. But not for long. The passengers for whose conduct to their destination he was responsible found their progress suddenly arrested and its direction reversed. The train went backwards

17

and stopped, and all on board, when the situation had been explained to them, began a search for the missing dentures, which was finally and deservedly successful.

How many of us would have been capable of this degree of moral courage? If we had dropped a baby out of a train, or a rare first edition of some well-known book, or a casket of jewels, or a portfolio crammed with secret papers, we should, no doubt, have nerved ourselves to take the action which the engine-driver took; but to hold up a startled trainload of complete strangers and to set them searching upon the broad bosom of Mother Nature for one's false teeth, that really must have taken a nerve. Some of us, it is greatly to be feared, might have thought twice about doing it even if we had been driving a freight train.

NAMES MUSHROOMIC

An unusually belated season being over, peace has just returned to those cautious but curious (and greedy) explorers of the early morning fields who annually torture themselves with the thought that, through not really knowing a mushroom from a toadstool, they are missing good things. For those of us who are frankly too much afraid of breakfasting with the Borgias to eat a fungus of our own picking, the adventurous amateur is an object of mingled admiration and pity. He is a cross between an inquiring and inexpert botanist and a pig rooting for truffles. Nothing is more restful to the unashamedly ignorant than to watch the botanist as she pounces on some insignificant little flower in a south country copse and asserts excitedly that she has seen its coloured picture in her book at home. The mounting tale of previous disappointments behind her is forgotten and, having picked or even dug up her victim, she returns to match it against the picture which, nine times out of ten, proves to be of some plant only—and rarely at that —seen in the Highlands.

Mushroomers, similarly at sea, have the added burden of being tempted to back their fancy by eating it and, like the wild flower huntswomen, they muddle themselves with print and illustrations. Seen there, the difference between edible and poisonous is plain enough. Fungi with gills sinuate and decurrent, adnate and adnexed, fall into simply recognized groups, varying in culinary charm from unexcelled in flavour, though rather indigestible, to causing intense suffering, followed by death. Unfortunately, the ringleader of some nine varieties to be avoided is common in woods and, by comparison with others, looks rather friendly. Its name—Death Cap—

19

better fits that sinister Fly Agaric, with its slimy scarlet cap covered with yellowish warts, which may yet be eaten in small quantities with nothing worse than an intoxicating effect. Panther Cap has the decency to give off an unpleasant, sickly smell, but its alias of False Blusher, earned because it can so readily be mixed up with the harmless Blusher, betrays a depth of treachery matched by Crested Lepiota, who combines the scent of a radish and an appealing fragility with more anti-social behaviour. Livid Entoloma and Red-staining Inocybe unblushingly look their evil parts, but Verdigris Agaric, which, with its bluish-green hue in youth looks worse, suggesting the most violent gastronomic consequences, has found one continental writer (whose intrepidity is not recommended for imitation) to label it as eatable.

When the eye turns to the more pleasant side of the picture and contemplates the nineteen or so edible mushrooms, admiration must go out to the pioneers who first charted this treacherous course. Who first dared to get his teeth into Shaggy Caps or the Tawny Grisette? Who, meeting a Parasol, plain or ragged, took it home to his wife and persuaded her to cook it? Remember, he may have said, how poorly you thought of Blewits and of Oyster fungi and how you sneeringly remarked that the fairies who danced among the Fairy Ring Champignons must have been bad ones from their Titania downwards. Have you forgotten your cry of horror on being invited to slice that ugly looking brute the Chanterelle and to fry it lightly before stewing it in stock until the latent tenderness emerged? If ever there was a wicked toadstool in appearance the Saffron Milk Cap is one, but recall how good it is baked. So the pioneer pursued his way, gathering Giant Puffballs to be served like cutlets, singing the praises of the grotesquely shaped Ceps, the Rough-Stalked Boletus and the honey-combed Morel. The poor woman must have been so bewildered at the end that she would have mashed Death

20

Cap itself for the children's lunch and insisted on second helpings all round. Or was she? Browsing among what MEREDITH, coining a phrase for another purpose, called " names mushroomic," the timid *gourmet* will couple, with his vote of thanks to the first man who tasted some of these mushrooms, another toast. It will be to the long forgotten dog or other animal, on whom the enigmatic plant was tried.

NUISANCE VALUE

It is clear that one man's sport may be another man's nuisance. Not long ago some of those living near complained to the Courts of the noise of a speedway racing track, though it was doubtless the most exquisite music to its local fans. Then a lady resented being struck on the head by a cricket ball hit magnificently out of the ground. Now there comes from Sydney the story of a plaintiff who objected to the defendant's racing pigeons —only 350 of them, as the defence gently protested. They " bustled and cooed in their lofts as is the wont of pigeons " ; they made a mighty whirring and they aroused the plaintiff and her husband with ruthless punctuality at dawn—at least so the plaintiff averred. The defendant, on the other hand, said they would not have been tiresome if the plaintiff had not frightened them by letting off crackers. The judge seems to have thought that this was no more than a natural act of retaliation and held that the pigeons were a nuisance. It is easy to feel for both sides. Anyone who on the first day of the Olympic Games saw the great flight of pigeons will remember how they made the loveliest silvery pattern against the black background of the stands before rising over the top to vanish into the blue sky. Recalling that magical moment he will sympathize with the pigeons, but to be called by them every day at dawn does seem rather too much of a good thing. The " three jolly pigeons " of which Tony Lumpkin sings so engagingly in the play might be capital fun, but 350 of them would make for too much jollity.

Perhaps the hard truth is this : there are all manner of sounds belonging to different sports which are delightful to their respective votaries ; yet to those who do not care for these things they mean nothing and if too often repeated would drive them into a madhouse. That of the bat meeting the ball, so distinctive in its solemn richness, seems to many people an essential part of a summer day's beauty. The thud of an invisible football heard through the misty air ; the rattle of the tennis ball on the penthouse ; most characteristic of all perhaps the continuous machine-gun fire of a long row of fives courts—all these things can be heavenly and romantic beyond words. Yet even those who love them might jib every now and then at mornings full of the pigeons' wings. What is music to me is but a noise to another and a beastly noise at that. It was only the other day that the neighbours—it is always the neighbours who are so hard-hearted—positively objected to the crooner in a restaurant orchestra. After that who shall predict the vagaries of taste ?

PORTRAIT OF HARRY

Practically everybody knows that it is bad luck to use a real mirror as part of a stage setting; but too few dramatists realize the inauspicious consequences that can flow from their decision to introduce, as an integral adjunct of the plot, a portrait of one of the characters. This is practically always a portrait in oils; and it has to be of the very largest size, so that the people in the cheap seats can see what it is meant to be. It is virtually a bye-rule of dramaturgy that we get a sight of the portrait before the character who is supposed to have sat for it is brought upon the stage, for it is normally used as a sort of preview or trailer designed to heighten our interest in the original. This device is, technically, invaluable to the dramatist. The portrait, hanging there upon the wall, gives everybody in the cast the opportunity to indicate their feelings towards the sitter. They can sigh at it, rolling their eyes with devotion; it can cause them to shudder or to shake their fists; and nothing more surely invites to soliloquy, provided the stage-manager has solved the difficult problem of hanging the picture in a place where the audience can see it and the actors can address it without turning their backs on the audience.

These are undoubted conveniences, and all might in practice be well if only the dramatist were prepared to admit that the portrait is a very bad portrait. This fact is strikingly evident to the front rows of the stalls, who would not find it (as they do) objectionable and distracting if everybody on the other side of the footlights were not so blind to it. If only the old Duke, gazing mistily upwards at the atrociously executed likeness of his long lost heir, would let it be known that Harry's portrait had been painted (as indeed appears to be the case) by the estate

24

carpenter, to humour the old man, nobody would think any the worse of Harry—and nobody could think any the worse of the picture—than they do already. But no, there is not a chance of any such concession to realism. " I remember it so well," says the lovely visitor. " It was the picture of the year, wasn't it ? " Or " Dubonnet always swears he never did anything better," Harry's uncle insists on informing us. It is not surprising that after a bit the frightful daub begins to get on the nerves of those of us who have a good view of it.

If the artistic drawbacks to stage portraits are not recognized by dramatists as valid, one would expect them to be impressed by the purely practical problems which they raise. What happens when the leading actor is indisposed and an understudy takes the part of Harry ? Has the portrait got an understudy too, or do the actors have to put in new lines—" We must expect to notice changes in him after all this time " and that sort of thing ? And finally, why put such a formidable obstacle in the way of the amateur dramatic societies, who are capable of yielding a respectable crop of royalties ? They can produce plenty of actors who can' at least have a sporting shot at playing Harry, but it is rather much to expect them to throw up an artist capable of painting an enormous portrait of the performer who gets the part ; and the line " Dubonnet always swears he never did anything better " will be fraught with even more than its usual implausibility for an audience in which every one knows that the vicar's sister was responsible for the ghastly exhibit.

BOFFINS OF THE COOKHOUSE

Fantastic though it now seems, there was a time when rations were things that only soldiers were expected to live on. Though generally understood to be frugal and unappetizing, they had in the eyes of civilians a certain rude glamour, and the sort of people who believed that our brave lads really rather enjoyed being under canvas and took a positive pleasure in cleaning their rifles also supposed that to subsist on rations constituted a masochistic sort of privilege. All that has changed now, many people believing—though few liking to say—that army rations are gargantuan compared with their own and that it would do some of those hulking young fellows a world of good to stand in a fish queue every now and then. It is to be feared that this attitude of mind will have gained ground as a result of a recent competition organized at Aldershot by the Army Catering Corps training centre. Entries in this culinary joust included a number of ambitious *plats* well beyond the scope of a law-abiding housewife who, though she might have managed a pair of dice, could hardly have confected a whole chess-board out of pressed beef and in whom the urge to fashion a dart-board out of fillets of sole has constantly to be repressed.

In these days the fish in her shopping-basket are in inverse ratio to the chips on the housewife's shoulder, and men are likely to take a more tolerant view of this slightly *recherché* evidence that the General Staff are trying to improve the standard of cooking throughout the Army. Those with military experience will tend to regard the whole thing with a certain scepticism. It is not that they doubt the sincerity of the Army Council's desire to provide all ranks with appetizing victuals. The importance of food has long been a tenet of British military thought, and many a young officer, asked by his instructor what he would do in some imaginary (but always dreadfully awkward) tactical situation, has gained valuable time by replying no less firmly than promptly : " Give the men a hot meal, sir." Like the question " Have you stopped beating your wife ? " this response always puts the pundits in a slightly false position. It is seldom possible for them to prove that the men would not, at this particular juncture, be all the better for a hot meal ; and any attempt to do so, or to suggest that their commander would have other and more urgent duties to perform, lays them open to all sorts of charges and casts grave doubt (or enables grave doubt to be cast) on their capacity as regimental officers.

Nobody, not even the most hare-brained subaltern or the most eccentric major, has ever varied this time-honoured formula by saying " Give the men a good meal." People would think he was trying to be funny or had gone mad. It is tacitly recognized that the very best that can be hoped for a meal—on active service, at any rate—is that it should be hot. The duty officer, going his rounds at dinner time, knows better than to call out " Any compliments for the chef ? " What he asks is " Any complaints ? " He has been asking it all down the ages, and in JULIUS CAESAR's day the picquet-centurion is more likely to have prefaced his inquiry with *nonne* than with *num*. So it may still be some time before the Army Catering Corps succeed in turning all our soldiers into sybarites ; and the fact that their succulent exhibits at Aldershot were dominated by " a replica of Nelson's column carved in rock salt," although doubtless intended as a delicate compliment to the Senior Service, suggests that virtuosity may still leave the duty officer some awkward objections to deal with.

TWIN SOLDIERS

Comparatively few people have had any experience of being a twin. They can therefore hardly appreciate a twin's feelings on hearing that the SECRETARY of STATE for WAR will allow him to join the same unit on the same date and undergo his whole-time Army service with his brother. It seems just possible, though to be sure we who are not twins cannot tell, that he may find this concession rather disappointing than otherwise. After some years at school he has come near to attaining an identity of his own ; he has almost exhausted the tiresome jokes of his tactless masters and grown accustomed to being called Dum or Dee (the Tweedle being silent) by his young companions. He thought he was going to say " Goodbye to all that " and now it has got to begin all over again with a new series of worse jokes, and a sergeant-major, far cruder and more offensive than any school master, to make them. Those who have identical twins under their charge can be driven to extreme measures, as was Harry Graham's callous nurserymaid.

> O'er the rugged mountain's brow
> Clara threw the twins she nursed,
> And remarked " I wonder now
> Which will reach the bottom first."

Goodness knows what a sergeant-major might do in a moment of exasperation.

It can only be suggested by way of comfort to this agitated twin that he turn from Ruthless Rhymes to the Lays of Ancient Rome. Here is the best and most cheering precedent for military twins—

> So like they were, no mortal
> Might one from other know :
> White as snow their armour was :
> Their steeds were white as snow.

28

There can be nobody having ever had within his breast the heart of a boy and not of a monster, who has not loved the Great Twin Brethren for their interposition, unfair and unscrupulous though it was, on the Roman side in the battle of Lake Regillus. With what unearthly lustre their armour gleamed and with what unearthly speed did their horses come " pricking towards the town "! Nowhere is that boyish magic more compelling and enchanting. But, of course, the twin may not in the least need comforting, and will be delighted to have his brother with him. Indeed on second thoughts that is by far the most likely result. And after all, taking the lowest point of view, a twin must often be invaluable in an evasion of penalties by establishing a cast-iron alibi.

THE LADY AND THE HOWITZER

A dislike of bangs, though fairly general throughout the human race, is not universal. Sappers, for instance, like bangs very much, and their intellectual countenances light up like turnips at Hallowe'en when they are given the opportunity of detonating a charge—the bigger the better—of high explosive. The Chinese, so silent, so inscrutable, so deprecating, are passionately devoted to noise in all its forms, and lost no time (or fewer centuries, anyhow, than anyone else) in inventing gunpowder, so as to be able to gratify their taste for sounds louder and more violent than even their most powerful musicians could produce. Small boys like bangs in moderation, and while away much time which might otherwise be wasted by firing with cap-pistols at their infant sisters or at the cat or indeed at nothing at all. Even the elderly, even the practically gun-shy, enjoy the detonation of rockets which hardier souls have caused to rush up into the night sky above them and spangle it with pretty, ineffectual stars.

The majority of us, however, while stoically accepting the fact that our planet is a place on which bangs are bound to occur, hope that most (and would like to think that all) of them will be made in places which we ourselves do not frequent. We should detest the idea of a bang, and a very loud bang at that, occurring at regular intervals immediately outside our place of residence ; and with FRAU SCHNELLE, of Frankfurt, to whom this has been happening for some time, we are bound to feel considerable sympathy. FRAU SCHNELLE lives immediately opposite the United States Army Headquarters, in front of which a piece of ordnance is discharged every day at sunrise and sunset, possibly to call the attention of the citizens to these interesting though not unusual phenomena. FRAU SCHNELLE complains that these ceremonial explosions are bad for her nerves, her crockery and her aged mother and that moreover they are often unpunctual. The American commander has courteously undertaken to lessen the charge in what he calls the " salute howitzer " in order to " reduce its shock effect to a minimum."

This means, or should mean, that FRAU SCHNELLE will no longer be practically blown out of bed in the morning, an inconvenience which she claims to have suffered hitherto. But a detonation, however modulated, is still a detonation. Each sunrise, each sunset will still be greeted with a bang, and if FRAU SCHNELLE should for any reason wish to seek the bubble reputation, she is exceptionally, in fact uncomfortably, well placed to do so. Gratifying though it may be for potentates, when they go visiting, to receive the salvoes to which protocol entitles them—from the mere three guns granted to sheikhs in the Persian Gulf to the twenty-one guns which welcome foreign Sovereigns and the SULTAN OF ZANZIBAR— FRAU SCHNELLE can hardly be expected to feel the same way about the 730 bangs a year which she gets. The reflection, if it occurs to her, that even the SULTAN OF ZANZIBAR would have to pay more than thirty state visits before he heard an equivalent number of blanks discharged cannot be much consolation ; and really the only comfort the poor lady can find is in the thought that, if she had occupied a similar position outside a British headquarters, it might have been bagpipes.

THE SQUIRE OF WHITEHALL

It is not in sociological terms that we should interpret the announcement that "The Minister of Works is prepared to receive applications for the post of Game-keeper." Feudal though its echoes are, it does not imply any change of heart in the members of a Labour Government whose personal ambitions can hardly be supposed to tend towards squirearchy, for if they did they would hardly have made things quite so difficult for the squires. Still, even though the MINISTER OF WORKS has only made the announcement on behalf of his department (and cannot, therefore, when he says "an official residence will be available," be charged with personally transgressing the party line about tied cottages), this staid manifesto from Whitehall has several points of interest.

Not the least of these is the fact that it appears in *Horse and Hound*, thus creating something of the same effect as an advertisement for a butcher's boy inserted in a periodical devoted to the vegetarian cause. Applicants, it is boldly stated, must be able to "cope effectively with all types of vermin," a formula from which readers of *Horse and Hound* can draw only one conclusion, and that very terrible. It is true that the keeper is needed for Richmond Park, which has not been regularly hunted for some time; but that scarcely lessens the temerity of appealing, in a journal inseparably connected with fox-hunting, for a gamekeeper who will be required to put foxes down. Although the Minister's advertisement is four or five times as long as any of the others in the "Situations Vacant and Wanted" column, it is not on the score of its prolixity that the taxpayer—always a bit sceptical about the ways in which the Government may spend his money on publicity—will chiefly criticize it.

32

What he will be most likely to feel (and not for the first time) is a mild surprise that Whitehall knows so little about England.

MEASLES ON ICE

However unpleasant it may be for the men themselves, the news that eight members of the crew of the John Biscoe, now battling her way south through polar gales to relieve an Antarctic expedition, have gone down with measles is bound to seem faintly derisory. Measles are not, it must be admitted, among the most heroic complaints. We armchair explorers who do our journeying in the books of better and braver men have long ago established a pretty strict canon of what is permissible in this respect. We allow—indeed we expect—our heroes to suffer, but they must suffer from the right diseases. In the jungle malaria is *de rigueur* and snake-bite respectable but not, we insist, hay-fever. In the desert sunstroke and thirst add a necessary touch of drama, but if the intrepid fellows also suffer from rheumatism or indigestion—both highly inconvenient when riding on a camel—we expect them to keep quiet about it. So polar explorers may lose an ear or two from frost-bite or contract scurvy if they have forgotten their orange-juice, but measles . . .? No.

The news is likely to shatter yet another illusion. At those moments when the book falls from our knees and we find ourselves, like Walter Mitty, wondering whether we should lead our next expedition to the Pole or have another shot at finding the source of the Limpopo as the Prime Minister has kindly suggested, this question of disease plays an important part. Even in day-dreams a certain honesty lingers and reminds us that while we do not by any means like the cold we are also not noted for activity in the heat. And would a man who makes the most of the slightest indisposition really be fitted for struggling through fever-ridden forests with a tempera-

34

ture of 104 degrees ? The Poles, however—for this purpose it hardly matters which as we have not the slightest intention of going to either—are a different matter. They are cold, yes, but healthy. Have we not read that no germs survive to contaminate the polar air ? Rousing ourselves to poke the fire and pour another glass of sherry we already feel the glow of perfect health and the blood coursing through our veins.

Now, it seems, this is not necessarily true. Even if the John Biscoe took on board its particular measle while loading at some temperate port, it is disturbing to find the germ flourishing among the ice-floes of the Antarctic Continent. It is a poor consolation to know that the ship can hardly be more in quarantine than she is already or that there is no one to whom the disease can be given except a handful of penguins. Nor can the John Biscoe be the best place to enjoy measles as measles should be enjoyed—for instance, in the school sanatorium or, better still, at home during the last days of the holidays. The more we think of it the more unpleasant it appears. As we go in to dinner we have the firm step of a man who has made up his mind : it will be the Limpopo after all. Already we hear the grunts of the native boys as they shoulder their loads and disappear into the bush.

CARVING

" Carving," says the encyclopaedia, " is one of the oldest forms of artistic expression." The media in the author's mind were wood and stone, but the thoughts of the preoccupied reader at this season of the year will fly perhaps first to flesh and fowl and to carving for the table, which after all is art enough, and old enough, and frequently accompanied by words and gestures that are not inexpressive. Carving in this sense, like the driving of fours-in-hand, has suffered a decline among us. Smaller families and smaller joints began it, and rationing has still further reduced the opportunities for a deft exercise of the art. Christmas will increase the carver's scope, but only temporarily. The old hand, gratefully grasping the chance to show off, will be fortunate if he does not discover that lack of practice and the passage of the years have robbed him of some of his cunning. Younger men, lacking that thorough training which their forebears had, will find the season far too short for a proper apprenticeship. " Have you learned to carve ? " LORD CHESTERFIELD inquired in one of those letters to his son. " Do you use yourself to carve *adroitly* and genteelly, without hacking half an hour across a bone, without bespattering the company with the sauce, and without overturning the glasses into your neighbours' pockets ? " These awkwardnesses, as his lordship pointed out, are extremely disagreeable and easily avoided—but then there was something to work on in those days, at least in the circles in which his lordship's son was accustomed to dine. A man could take pride in his carving ; and a hundred years went by, after the writing of that letter, before the members of the Athenaeum ceased to carve for themselves and consented, under protest, to let a professional do it for them.

A great many households still are blessed with a hand that can wield a pretty carving knife, but how many other English castles there are with a youngish master whose youth was so ill spent that he knows all about landmines and nothing about turkeys. Two courses are open to this unfortunate. He may study those well-meant diagrams in the cookery textbooks and subsequently learn at the table how unrelated are some forms of literature to life ; or—magnanimous surrender—he may leave the carving to his wife, who learned the knack, maybe, when he was at the wars and has found it best to retain this department of household management in her own hands in the frugal days of peace. Husbands who follow this easy way out have been known to feel twinges of conscience, not on their wives' behalf, but because, they fear, they are letting the men's side down and opening the way to new assaults on masculine privilege. They should not worry unduly. It is not a new heresy they are guilty of ; there are worthy precedents for it. That good, long-suffering woman, the wife of the Vicar of Wakefield, did all the carving at dinner, " it being her mother's way." And so did the wife of Archbishop Benson. " My mother always carved instead of my father," Mr. E. F. Benson told us. " This was rather daring, rather modern, but she carved with swift artistic skill and he did not, and she invariably refused the offer of her neighbouring gentlemen to relieve her of her task." Those neighbouring gentlemen, one fancies, were a little disconcerted ; nowadays, perhaps, they would only be relieved.

STRANGER IN OUR MIDST

A bill of reckoning headed " Man in account with Giant Panda," would be hard to balance. On the one side, as shown by the quick and bumper response to the appeal for bamboo shoots, men are eager to behave hospitably to their conscribed guest, and she and her predecessor, Ming, have been loaded with admiration, and all manner of flattering attentions. When the panda, after centuries spent in the shy seclusion of its oriental mountain home, first became familiar to western naturalists it was called by one of them the most beautiful of all known quadrupeds. Beautiful is not, perhaps, the word chosen by crowds at the Zoo and in the toy shops, but no creature, since the teddy-bear won his way into childish and grown-up hearts, has given more delight. Here was a picture out of the nursery books come to life ; shape, markings, furry charm, and engaging manners combined in this Chinese highlander to provide a rival for the most imaginative animal painter in fiction or fairy tale.

Unfortunately, the giant panda, unlike the pobble, cannot live on an airy diet of praise. His tastes are simple and even austere, for, although he is a carnivore in shape, he is strictly, so far as he has been watched in his native haunts, a vegetarian, happily searching with those two lovely black eyes for bamboo and handling it, when found, with a delicacy of table manners that seem surprising from such long unwieldy-looking claws. Contentment with this fare is not asking for much, but there are, it seems, bamboos and bamboos, and those grown here may lack the vitamins of Tibet. Poor Ming, who made her bow in Regent's Park on a Christmas Eve just before the war, died in her sleep, six years later, on

Boxing Day, and now, and for the same reasons of imperfect nutrition, Lien Ho is on the sick list. The kindly donors who have rallied to her aid will, it may be hoped, see her through these midwinter hard times, but, without being sentimental, some men will ask themselves, rather guiltily, whether her ordeal was really necessary. Giant pandas have had, admittedly, to put up with worse than a cage made as comfortable and as healthy as zoological knowledge and friendly intentions can contrive. There are accounts from the past of skins and " specimens " changing hands and, as late as the period between the wars, a white man earned the unenviable distinction of being the first of his kind to shoot a giant panda. Collecting, except of the live animal, could no longer be done with public approval here or in America, but would the same feelings be aroused by any future expedition to replenish western zoos ?

The answer to that question must depend partly on how the wider issue of keeping wild animals in captivity is viewed. A small and single-minded minority sets its face against all cages and even against the partial freedom of a Whipsnade. Scientific opinion, which goes with reasoned kindness, points out in reply that animals survive in good condition and in many cases breed in a well-run zoo and that there is no evidence to suggest that they pine as they would do were they human. Between these two approaches comes that of most people who enjoy a visit to the Zoo, delight in escorting children from house to house, and yet, as they watch the restless lions pacing to and fro and the eagles perched motionless with wire netting between them and the skies, wonder whether such incarceration is justified as being educative and a legitimate satisfaction of curiosity about natural history. Twinges of conscience are felt less often and less acutely where the captives have plenty of room and can exist in the open air, and the modern tendency is to keep as many of them as possible out of cages. A game reserve being impracticable in Britain, Whipsnade is the next best thing, and the bigger the flow of migrants from London the easier it will be to satisfy the doubters. Change of quarters being unlikely to help the giant panda, is there not a case, now that he has been seen, to leave him undisturbed where nature put him and where, apparently, he has no enemies except the snow leopard?

THANK YOU, THANK YOU

King Lear may have been right when he exclaimed
> How sharper than a serpent's tooth it is
> To have a thankless child !

Many mothers, and not a few nannies, whose pride and joy stands scowling at its hostess's calves (round which a howling draught from the open front door savagely whips her skirts) and refuses to say " Thank you for the nice party," know exactly how King Lear felt. But it is not much fun, either, having a child whose energies are temporarily diverted into being thankful. Just as every rose has a thorn, so every Christmas present from the outside world involves a letter of thanks. Most children, though prepared to recognize—on an academic plane— the justice of this, takes a good deal of convincing, when the time comes, that in their own case justice really needs to be done. On Christmas morning, up to their hocks in coloured paper and shavings, they were full of good intentions and the spirit of reciprocity. When their mother exclaimed " But how kind of Aunt Griselda ! You must write her a specially nice letter ", it was with true sincerity that they echoed " Yes, I must." But that was a long time ago now. They still think well of Aunt Griselda's generosity, but there are better things to do than sit down and write her a letter. Besides, aren't they going to see her at the pantomime next week ? As for the old gentleman who sent them the long book by SHAKESPEARE, they don't even know him, at least they can't remember what he looks like. Surely you ought not to write to people whom you do not know ?

When at last these quibbles have been disposed of formidable administrative problems present themselves. Ruled paper, so indispensable at this stage of the

41

letter-writer's development, is less plentiful at home than at school ; and when it has been found a certain impetuosity in the scribe's approach to the task in hand results in ink being upset, often in quantities large enough to necessitate a partial change of clothing. Household words like " dynamo " and " conjuring tricks " take on strange and unfamiliar forms when committed for the first time to paper, creating an urgent demand for an eraser which, if met, results in the missive being savagely excoriated. There is nothing very cursive about the whole operation.

Bowed like a galley slave over his oar, the child ploughs its lonely furrow with an air of malevolent concentration. The desk bears what the police would describe as " signs of a struggle " ; and, indeed, a struggle is being waged—a struggle with the outposts of the English language, with the spatulescent nib, with little tarns of ink, with an intense desire to go and do something else, and—sooner or later—with ultimate truth. For there is a tendency for these letters of thanks to stereotype themselves. The child feels that what it has once said well it will never say better, and the phrase (used with perfect sincerity to Aunt Griselda) " It was just what I wanted " recurs throughout the whole correspondence. Of some presents it is true, of others it might be true, but of others again (and a glance at its innumerable but unillustrated pages strongly suggests that the book by SHAKESPEARE comes into this category) this statement is neither true nor even, in the child's view, credible. A doubt assails it ; its conscience is pricked. But what else is there to say ? " It was very nice " ? Lukewarm, and will not get you over the page. " I am going to read it as soon as I can " ? A blacker lie than the first. In the end the path of least resistance is taken. Down goes the well tried, the specious, the deceitful formula—" It is just what I wanted " ; and the child rises from the thankless task of being thankful with a stain on—among other things—its candour.

POTATOES AT MIDNIGHT

People who complain that the Civil Service is dilatory would do well to study a form which reached farmers in this country on or about New Year's Eve. It is an unusually small form, its modest acreage not exceeding that of an ordinary sheet of note-paper. To make up for this it is exceptionally well-found in the matter of reference numbers. E.G.49/5/S, which appears in four different places, is probably the one to conjure with at the Ministry of Food, from whose Potato and Carrot Division the form originated. But E.S. and S.51-6186 also appear, and some forms are embellished with 11/13/85, to say nothing of the mystic figure 24, printed twice very large. These cryptic and proliferating symbols (several of which almost certainly mean something to someone) are, however, normal—part, as it were, of the protective colouring which a bureaucracy feels all the safer for assuming. What is abnormal is the atmosphere of urgency which pervades the whole communication.

It purports to have been printed on December 31, 1949 though as this was the day on which farmers received it there is some reason to fear that an excess of zeal has caused the Ministry of Food to commit one of the offences against which recipients are specifically warned—to wit, " knowingly or recklessly making a statement false in a material particular " on the form. The purpose of the form is to secure an answer (failure to give which within seven days is also an offence) to the following question : " How many tons of marketable ware potatoes grown by you which can be dressed over $1\frac{1}{2}$in. riddle do you estimate you have in stock on your farm(s) as at midnight, Saturday-Sunday, 31st December, 1949-1st January, 1950 ? " It is the words " as at midnight " and the

43

fact that they refer to New Year's Eve which brings out dramatically the sense of emergency, the wonderful blend of tautness and precision which characterizes the methods of the Ministry of Food. The Potato and Carrot Division has, we may safely presume, its experts, quiet, slow-spoken men from the backwoods of Surrey who know to within a month or two the time of year at which farmers lift the potatoes which they grow. To these, perhaps, it will have seemed unlikely that the number of tons of this nutritious root estimated by farmers to be stored on their farms would fluctuate appreciably between, say, sunset on Saturday, December 31, 1949, and dawn on Monday, January 2, 1950. There has for some time been a strongly marked tendency for the tonnage of potatoes held on a farm at dinner-time on a Saturday to be still there on the following morning, and even on the morning after that ; and this interesting trend has never been more strikingly demonstrated than at week-ends which coincided with the New Year.

These considerations have not lulled the Ministry of Food into *laissez faire*. Farmers are often rather vague people, and if they had been asked to return the stocks they held on (for instance) New Year's Day there might have been a terrible muddle, capable of jeopardizing the nation's diet for years to come. So out went the fiat, as brisk, peremptory and stimulating as the crack of a whip. One visualizes, up and down the country, farmers stumbling a shade unsteadily over their clamps as the church bells rang out the Old Year, doing rather specula-tive sums on their frozen fingers and wishing MR. STRACHEY all possible success with his ground-nuts.

44

SMALL GUESTS

Though easier to organize than (for instance) world peace, the large-scale cultivation of groundnuts and television programmes, children's parties nevertheless involve those who arrange them in problems of a certain magnitude. No one has ever been known to speak of " throwing " a children's party ; the hint of reckless, impulsive abandon would be altogether out of place. The logistics of these functions are formidable enough in themselves ; the provision of fare which will appear sumptuous without making the consumers sick, the need to place cushions on many of the chairs so that the junior guests can get at the stuff, the selection of presents which will not seem to some recipients an insult to their years or to others incomprehensible and alarming, the emergency measures designed to cope with the more drastic effects of over-eating—these and many other purely material problems weigh heavily on the hostess, and are sometimes rather unfairly allowed to affect the host's peace of mind.

Then there are the *bouches inutiles*, the grown-ups, whose detested presence is sometimes made necessary either because their own entries need supervision or because they have not (or so they allege) enough petrol to go all the way home and come back again after tea. They have to be fed and provided with ash-trays in unlikely places—though by an unwritten law they need not be given chairs, a laughing injunction to " find somewhere to sit," perhaps accompanied by a small gesture like those made by Chinese stage hands when dressing the stage with imaginary furniture, being all that convention requires of the hostess. Finally, there is the question, which has never been conclusively solved—and seldom, indeed,

45

seriously tackled—by sociologists, of where to sequester the conjurer until it is time for him to do his stuff.

The real trouble with children's parties, however, is the children. Without them the whole business could be approached with a reasonable degree of confidence. Though less easily bored than grown-ups, children resemble their elders in that while some throw themselves with delightful enthusiasm into social activities others do nothing of the sort. Though seldom behindhand as trenchermen, these, once the festive board has been cleared, tend to lose interest in the proceedings. Organized games leave them cold. At hide-and-seek their methods of concealment are either completely perfunctory or else so thorough that they disappear altogether and, obstinately refusing to call " Coo-ee," are supposed by the more impressionable type of hostess to have somehow converted themselves into a corpse and thus cause a mild panic. They do not shine at charades, walking through the increasingly unimportant parts allotted to them with an air of detached resignation. They are never numerous but always a nuisance. That slight scowl worries the hostess. It shows clearly that Cecil is not enjoying himself and it may mean that he is going to be sick. But the host, who secretly shares what appears to be Cecil's view of the proceedings, cannot find it in his heart to blame the anti-socialite, and reflects charitably that, just as all children's parties would be much more manageable if it were not for the children, so some children would be much more agreeable acquaintances if it were not for children's parties.

HAPPY SLUGGARD

Many people on reading of the various new arrivals at the Zoo must have felt an instant and instinctive sympathy with one species of whom they had probably never heard before. These are the European sousliks, some sort of cousins of the marmots, who, after not being seen here for fifty years, have now come from Austria to live in a pleasant enclosure specially made for them next door to the Rodent House. That which arouses our envy and admiration is that they "seem disinclined to stir from their burrows until at least two hours after sunrise." Could anything be more snug, more wise or more courageous ? The sun now rises soon after eight o'clock, so we may assume that it is about a quarter past ten at the earliest that the souslik rubs his eyes, reluctantly flings aside his blanket and peers cautiously out upon a wintry world. His views coincide to a great extent with those of CHARLES LAMB when he protested at being told to rise with the lark. "For a mere human gentleman," he said, "we take ten, or half after ten (eleven of course during the Christmas solstice) to be the very earliest hour at which he can begin to think of abandoning his pillow." What the souslik does in summer we are not told ; perhaps we may make up some lost time on him then, if he still goes by the sun and we stick to our winter hours, but at present he has all the best of it. He gets up to a day that has been well aired and warmed for him, while some at any rate of us must rise while the moon still hangs in the sky, a little pale and faded and jaded like a lady going home after a late dance.

If it is a genuine virtue or a genuine necessity that prevents us from emulating this beautifully indolent little animal that is some comfort ; but very often it is mere

47

cowardice—partly fear of public opinion, partly a timid conservatism that insists day after day on walking the same seedy mill round and is terrified of breaking its own rules. We may still remember from school days some heroic figure who ever and anon quite simply refused to get up for early school. Having counted the the cost (probably a Georgic) he deliberately turned over and went to sleep again nor ever doubted afterwards that the indulgence had been worth the penalty. There is about such creatures a greatness of soul not given to most of us. There may be no compelling reason why we should get up, nothing but a vaguely uneasy conscience and an obedience to routine ; we may toy for a while with the notion of staying in bed, but we lack the true resolution ; and we get up at an hour that is neither one thing nor the other, make a guilty scramble of dressing, find the breakfast cold, and lose all pleasure in our truancy. The souslik is likewise, it appears, a creature of habit, but his is a brave and sensible habit. He is hanged if he will get up and he doesn't get up.

IT MIGHT BE WORSE

It is a curious thing that there is no recognized answer to the commonest question in the world. Almost every day and often several times a day we are asked how we are and nine times out of ten we are at a loss to know how to reply. Even if we could consciously decide, before setting out in the morning, that we felt very well or rather depressed or utterly miserable, the problem would not be solved. To announce that one is very ill is to demand sympathy unfairly ; to say that one is very well may seem a dangerous challenge to fortune. Over generations Englishmen have worked out a number of formulas that seem to provide a satisfactory escape from this dilemma. They may dodge it altogether by replying, somewhat feebly : " And how are you ? " ; they may take refuge in flippancy if they are of the flippant kind ; or they may say, quite truthfully, that things might be worse. The last of the three, with its variations of " Can't complain " and " Mustn't grumble," might be said to express the characteristic philosophy of the British nation so far as it is possible to do so in one sentence.

It is disappointing, therefore, to find this reply being quoted as evidence of unusual gloom. MR. ZEMANEK, the London Correspondent of the Czechoslovak Radio, in what seems to have been an unnecessarily depressing picture of the plight of the British people in 1950, said that " The usual answer to the question ' How are you ? ' was ' It could be worse.' " MR. ZEMANEK is quite right ; but since Englishmen have been saying this for goodness knows how long, it can hardly be proof of any sudden deterioration in the national fortunes. In a new democracy like Czechoslovakia, no doubt, it would be more truthful if hardly more discreet to reply " It could be better,"

D

but would it really be evidence of a more optimistic spirit?

Properly considered there is something rather magnificent in the phrase " It might be worse." If it had to be expanded it might run like this. " Here am I, a man like other men, with rather more health and rather less money than most—or the other way round—neither expecting nor deserving the smile of Fortune. Income-tax is nine shillings in the pound ; there is a depression approaching from the Azores ; and I have a bet on a horse which will infallibly lose. The Government is notoriously inefficient, but since Governments always are there is no reason for astonishment or indignation. I must certainly visit the dentist before the end of the month." Having completed this catalogue of disaster there is a certain satisfaction in coming to the conclusion, which MR. ZEMANEK may dislike but cannot deny, that " it might be worse "—and since it is a phrase which, in one form or another, has served very well from the Spanish Armada to the London blitz we are not likely to abandon it now.

GOING ROUND IN CIRCLES

Foreign correspondents often attribute the content of a dispatch to " usually well-informed circles," and there is something very striking about the phrase. The choice of adverb is peculiarly pregnant, contriving as it does simultaneously to affirm faith and to adumbrate doubt. It implies that the correspondent has found these circles to be reliable in the past, but it sounds at the same time a note of caution. " You know what these foreigners are," it seems to say ; " don't blame me if they've got hold of the wrong end of the stick this time." It suggests very strongly that the correspondent has, at some earlier stage of his career, been badly caught out. " Well-informed circles," perhaps he telegraphed from Strelsau, " predict with confidence that a decree nationalizing the tramways of Ruritania will be published next week " ; and perhaps on the basis of this message his editor launched a violent attack on the growth of totalitarianism in a country so closely associated in the minds of Englishmen with free and often desperate enterprise ; and then in the end nothing happened—the tramways were not nationalized, the Ruritanians simply went on running each other through the heart to the accompaniment of mocking laughter and the editor was made to look a fool. Never again thereafter did the correspondent quote well-informed circles without making it clear to his readers that they were only usually so.

There is no need to sneer at him for hedging in this (after all) only very slightly pusillanimous way. Most of us would be hard put to it to locate, let alone obtain the *entrée* to, any kind of a circle, even the most habitually deluded. In the old days persons of distinction or notoriety had circles of their own, and when they died their

51

biographers often included in the titles of their works some reference to these satellite institutions, which were then regarded as almost integral to their owner as his cat is to DICK WHITTINGTON. " Rossetti and His Circle," " Henry Irving and His Circle," " Mrs. Brookfield and Her Circle "—like children bowling hoops they effortlessly propel their entourage in front of them along the road to immortality. As a social phenomenon the circle presumably owes its origin to the camp-fires of our primitive ancestors. Although in those days preternaturally ill-informed, it was at least a circle ; and though it survived for many centuries the invention of the fireplace, which converted it into a semi-circle, the dawn of an age in which it became impermissible to speak of " the best circles " sounded its death-knell. Geometrically, of course, all circles are perfect ; but it is ridiculous to pretend that all circles are equal and in countries where there are no such things as the best circles it follows that there can be no circles at all.

This partly explains why none of us any longer has a circle, as ROSSETTI had his and MRS. BROOKFIELD hers. Another reason is that a circle, like a pack of hounds or a troupe of performing sea-lions, takes a lot of feeding. We may be the intellectual superiors of those earliest circles, squatting round their camp-fires, but though their conversation was doubtless beneath contempt they could at least say : " Here, have another bit of mammoth " or " After you with the bear's meat "—which is more than we can, *mutandis* never so much *mutatis*. It seems, in short, that the circle is as obsolete in society as the square is upon the battlefield which once it dominated. It is only abroad that it survives, but even there it is a little difficult to visualize ; and it is much to be hoped that, if ever the biography of a veteran foreign correspondent is entitled " Jones and His Usually Well-Informed Circle," it will be illustrated as profusely as possible.

THE ENGINE'S NAME

Comparatively few passengers take the trouble to walk up the platform and look at that noble monster of an engine that will soon be thundering with them over hill and dale ; and of those few by no means all observe its name. Yet there is no reason why the name of an engine should not be as romantic as that of a ship or give as much interest to a journey as does that of a public house that flits past the traveller's eye. So it is pleasant to read of something like a wholesale christening of engines—no plebeian drawers of goods trains, but express passenger engines of the highest birth—to sixty-eight of which the Railway Executive has just allotted names. Those not overfond of regimentation of any kind may have feared lest nationalization should produce a deadly uniformity with the engines distinguished by mere dull numbers. On the contrary the engines are not only to have names but names carrying on the tradition of the systems to which they would have belonged, had they been born a little earlier, and of their domicile of origin in the form of particular locomotive works.

Some of these names are eminently safe, sound, and solemn, such as those of Scottish cities and their patron saints. National birds such as guillemots and curlews similarly represent a policy of playing for safety. There could be no possible complaints. Other names are more enterprising and may give rise to a general knowledge paper among the passengers. Fame is a glorious thing, but it lasts all too short a time and even the names of military commanders grow dim. Of all the motorists who on a certain leafy Kentish road pass a house entitled " The Sir Jeffrey Amherst " how many could recount that hero's victories ? Even our knowledge of the Marquis

OF GRANBY, though he may be technically immortal, is general rather than particular. And so this wave of oblivion may pass over the names of the most eminent locomotive engineers. " Daddy," the small boy will ask, as he gazes at the engine," who was Alexander Sturrock ? " and his father will have no resource but to say that it is time to get back into their carriage. Even race horses, who have also given their names to engines, may be almost forgotten. When exactly did Bois Roussel win the Derby ? As to Scottish Union, who didn't, he may some day be confused with a political amalgamation. We may hope that at least SIR WALTER SCOTT is safe with Marmion and Guy Mannering, and yet it could have been wished that Dandie Dinmont had enjoyed the honour awarded to that rather tiresome eponymous colonel. He had his own simple system of names. " There's auld Pepper and auld Mustard, and young Pepper and young Mustard, and little Pepper and little Mustard. That's a fancy of my ain to mark the breed." The Railway Executive has shown a more extensive fancy and next time perhaps it will give Dandie a turn.

SUCH A STIR

Publishers are sometimes impelled (though never frequently enough to please their authors) to advertise their books in the newspapers. On these occasions their technique appears to be governed by some kind of a code which, though dictated rather by prudence than by modesty, makes their excursions into publicity seem shy, genteel little outings compared with the reverberant campaigns of other advertisers. Few publishers, for instance, possess the nerve which enables film magnates to describe any forthcoming production as stupendous, or colossal, or uniquely dynamic. They do, indeed, hope most sincerely that this is how their book will strike the better-known reviewers ; and if this happens the trickiest of their advertising problems (which is what, apart from the book's title and the author's name, to put in the advertisement) is automatically solved. If the industrious Mr. Puff or the revered Miss Plume go into ecstasies over the book, or even apply to it one or two favourable epithets which can be extracted like plums from a crusty context, the publisher need worry no longer. " Its power is undeniable " : O. K. Puff. " Plangent with integrity " : Nebula Plume. " An unusual tale " : *The Kirkcudbright Intelligencer*—excerpts such as these provide the publisher's advertisement with a *modus vivendi* which is almost a *raison d'être*.

These invaluable quotations, however, cannot in the nature of things become available until after the work and the critics' verdicts on it have been published. It is the book which the publisher deems important enough to advertise before publication date that tests his advertising ability most severely. Experience, one presumes, has taught him that he alone of advertisers cannot expect the public to attach credence to any high-flown and extravagant claims which he himself may make on behalf of his own product. If he were selling soap or beer or patent medicines no inhibition would deter him from describing his wares as ideal, or the best in the world, or indispensable to true happiness ; but something must warn him that similar statements by a publisher about a book would be taken no more seriously than if they had been made by the wretched author (who, if he advertised his own book as a jolly good one, would instantly be condemned as a charlatan and a bounder). Few publishers, at any rate, are unduly lavish with their eulogies of forthcoming volumes.

Every now and then, however, one makes a desperate effort to impress on the public his own high opinion of a book by blowing his trumpet in such a way as to produce—while appearing not to blow it at all—a long, low blast which will carry complete conviction. The latest publisher to essay this difficult feat does so by taking us behind the scenes and telling us what happened when the novel which he is advertising arrived at his place of business. " It caused," he tells us, " such a stir in the publisher's office that production was held up while the original copy passed from hand to hand among the staff." As the novel (we are also told) is 640 pages long, production must have been held up for some considerable time. If we assume that his staff numbers twenty and that each took an average of three working days to wade through the 640 deathless pages, we get a vivid idea of how disastrous can be the impact of genius upon productivity. Even more vivid—for anyone familiar with the interior of a modern publishing house—is the scene evoked by the words " production was held up." From the vast boilers in the engine-room only a wisp of steam emerges ; the rhythmical *tosh-tosh* of the great pulping machine is stilled ; mice, emboldened by the weeks of unaccustomed silence, gambol, unregarded upon the rusting conveyor-belt, while the staff—a long, orderly, expectant queue—await their turn to read a book which—as their employer has surely earned the right to say—" comes in the ' can't put it down ' class." Happy publisher ! Yet if every masterpiece submitted to him is going to bind his colleagues and subordinates in a spell so comprehensive and mesmeric he must (one cannot help feeling) entertain the hope that some of them, at any rate, will be a good deal less than 640 pages long. If not, he may have to consider arranging for the more gripping manuscripts to be read aloud to his assembled employees. It should then prove possible to resume production in a matter of days.

NEW BONES FOR OLD

The exact status of the skeleton which must (one imagines) have been present, on some now no longer identifiable occasion, at a feast has never been satisfactorily defined. The frequency with which one hears the phrase " a skeleton staff " suggests that it may have been operating as a waiter ; but feasts were feasts in those days and the gumless jaws intoning " Thick or clear, your Grace ? " the harsh grating sound which accompanied the stooping proffer of boar's head or of spinach, would probably have passed unnoticed in the haze of conviviality. The general consensus of opinion is that the skeleton must somehow have usurped the status of a guest. " Is that old So and So ? " one imagines a reveller inquiring. " Looks a bit fine drawn, doesn't he ? " And at length came the terrible discovery that the still figure at the end of the table was not old So and So—or anyhow not all of him.

Skeletons are also closely associated with cupboards, and if the contemporary feast offers the keen trencherman nothing much better than a walkover the contemporary cupboard is not a receptacle which, at the mere thought of its contents, sets the gourmet licking his lips. To come to the point, it is difficult to ascribe to an accident of fate the fact that an artificial skeleton has just been placed on the market, " at a price considerably less than the cost of the genuine article." Resistant as it is to rough handling, climatic variations and acids, this latest product of British craftsmanship can be supplied within two weeks of ordering and there is presumably none of the old trouble about getting spare parts of the right size. It can fairly be described as the young anatomist's *vade mecum*.

Though it will make life easier and less expensive for many deserving people, the new synthetic skeleton is not an unmixed blessing, like spam and egg-powder and de-hydrated radish extract. These substitutes do not lessen our respect for the viands for which they are supposed, somewhat fancifully, to be more than capable of deputizing, but real skeletons are bound to go down in the world and this—since every one of us is a bone-owner—is a matter which affects us all. The production on a commercial basis of false hair has been going on for a long time but fluctuations in the market thus created were not of equal concern to the whole community, for some were too old and others too young to have a saleable surplus of the genuine article, and moreover methods of cropping varied, especially among the female population, so widely and so unpredictably that project after project for state control of the hair trade has foundered on the jagged, ungraphed reefs of imponderability. Skeletons are a different matter. Every citizen, from the youngest to the oldest, from the spineless yes-man to the double-jointed contortionist, possesses one. " Fair shares for all " is not the goal ; it is the *status quo.* Any attempt, therefore, by uncontrolled private enterprise to dislocate the set of values which has hitherto been a Briton's death-right must arouse the detestation of all doctrinaires worthy of that name. It is to the political party which in the crisis of to-day will save not only our skin but our bones that the electorate will confide their suffrages.

CLOUD OVER CLUBLAND

There is probably no connexion between the Government's decision to close its hospitality centre in Mayfair and the PRESIDENT of the BOARD of TRADE'S reported request to London clubs to provide board and lodging for visitors from oversea. There is—if one may say so without disrespect—a certain air of inevitability about the Government's failure to run a hotel successfully, but MR. WILSON'S appeal to clubland is unexpected. The Board of Trade we know to be a versatile institution ; those who imagine it to be staffed entirely by hard-headed men who can think about nothing but jute are quite mistaken. Its influence on literature is far-reaching, for it controls both the import and the export of books ; until the other day it fixed the prices of timber, and thus played no small part in determining the future of our woodlands ; it dabbles extensively in films, it has a Production Efficiency Service and its senior officials include a hosiery controller, a tobacco adviser and a strong supporting cast ; but it had not hitherto been supposed to have a direct interest in getting (for instance) Esquimaux into the Cavalry Club.

The zeal of the Board of Trade in tackling this project is commendable ; but its access of vicarious hospitality may not arouse a corresponding impulse in the members of the clubs concerned. In most reputable clubs it takes several years before the inmates can train themselves to repress the shudder automatically generated by the sight of each new member ; and on some of the senior denizens the effect of finding a completely strange Afghan sitting in their favourite chair might well prove fatal. Clubs are, moreover, somewhat insular institutions, and a far-reaching overhaul of the amenities they provide would in many cases be necessary before the oversea visitors would feel at home. The inevitable demand for iced water might well gravel the house committee at Black's, where water of whatever temperature is not generally believed to possess the properties of a beverage ; and the lack of female society at the Athenaeum would arouse in millionaires from Latin America the traditional melancholy of their native pampas. The Chinese would miss their noodles at Boodle's, and their actors, though trained to dispense with real furniture on the stage, would soon get tired of reclining on imaginary sofas on days when there was a large attendance at the Garrick.

The whole plan bristles, in fact, with problems that will tax to the uttermost the *savoir-faire* of the staff of the Board of Trade, which numbers some 10,000 souls. The harsh and inescapable fact is that foreign visitors need somewhere to sleep. A good many hotels are requisitioned by Government departments and others are, or will be when the rush comes, full. The gaols are all bursting with delinquents, and many visitors would in any case misunderstand our motives if we tried to accommodate them in cells. So there are, presumably, only the clubs left ; and the members of Blank's, who can only by a superhuman effort conceal the loathing which they feel for the members of Dash's when they come to them for a month in the summer, must broaden their outlook, brace their wills and prepare to receive Bulgarians.

AT HENTY'S SHRINE

Many more or less elderly gentlemen must have experienced a variety of emotions on learning the taste in literature of the boy readers of Shoreditch between fourteen and eighteen. They may have felt sad, but reconciled to the fact, that the young gentlemen will not read SCOTT, pitied them for not liking " The Prisoner of Zenda," rejoiced that they do like " Treasure Island " and " Huckleberry Finn." They have perhaps borne up over Robinson Crusoe's decline, never having been very sound about him themselves, and as to what is apparently the most popular book of all, " The Saint," the old fogies may have to confess that they had never heard of it. But all such sentiments are mild and cool compared with the really heart-warming glow produced by the news of their once beloved HENTY ; he is " a great deal more popular than would be commonly thought " and there is a " regular consistent demand " for him. The thought of him brings back to them all manner of beautiful memories. There was the practical certainty, as Christmas drew near, of at least one brand-new Henty with a liberal splash of gilding on the cover. It more than compensated for the irritation of being annually and condescendingly addressed in the preface as " My dear lads." To some there may return a very particular vision. It is tea-time in the dining hall of a private school. The sound of the chumping of bread and butter is gradually dying away. Then there is heard from the dais a voice proclaiming " Those who have finished may read." Instantly, as if by a conjuring trick, some fifty or sixty Hentys are produced from nowhere and slapped down upon the table.

The curious thing about these elderly HENTY " fans "— that vulgarism was unknown in their young days—is that their affection is a purely sentimental and unreasoning one. They know better than to put it to a practical test by re-reading one of their old favourites. It is, indeed, one of the remarkable features of those works that the titles remain so clear and everything else is so dim. " In Times of Peril " was the Indian Mutiny and " By Sheer Pluck " Ashanti, " With Clive in India " and " The Young Carthaginians " explain themselves. " St. George for England " was surely Crécy, or was it by chance Agincourt? It is easy enough to reel off those lovely names, but what was it all about? Not so much as the ghost of an incident remains. Yet something does remain—namely, a little, a very little, history. There are some who can still recite with quite an air the names of the generals who fought against GUSTAVUS ADOLPHUS, from having once known " The Lion of the North." That may not be much, but it is something. To try to regain more would be rash, for it would probably be to lose all. There are certain books the re-reading of which is foolhardy in the extreme. Even dear CAPTAIN MARRYAT is dangerous. The jokes about Captain Goode's " beautiful white legs " have been known to pall in " King Solomon's Mines " though Gagool and the diamonds and the gorgeous fighting may carry the reader through. It is a dreadful moment for the browser in beloved old pastures when he feels a conviction that the charm has gone and that he is going to be bored. There is nothing for it but to shut up the book, instantly, tenderly, and for ever.

SUNDAY BEST

A pink donkey with green ears, standing on its head, has caused a mild flutter in church. Flutter is the word, for this gay, athletic animal added colour and interest to a scarf that, worn by a young lady at her devotions, may have distracted other people from theirs. If it did it was in the classic tradition of finery that, through the ages, has stood between the congregation and concentration on Sunday service. Easter was once the great day for new frocks and suits ; whole families from papa and mamma to the youngest member appeared as rivals to SOLOMON in all his glory. Underclothes, still retaining their pristine prickliness, might make the boys wriggle, but the *décor* as a whole was well—only too well—worth watching. As each unit marched up the aisle to its allotted pew, eyes right or left appraised the success of the season's domestic wardrobe. Those were the days when, in some families, only a Noah's ark could be played with on the Sabbath and light reading stopped short at " The Pilgrim's Progress." They were, it might seem, remote, but the gymnastic donkey on the scarf, so similar, in essence, to the spring bonnet that hinted suspiciously of having Paris as its spiritual home, brings them into kinship with the present.

Latest recruits to the ranks of the inattentive may fairly claim that a scarf, bearing a strange device, is no ordinary diversion. Even misogynists, so unobservant that they fail to notice what fashion has been up to with hats and hairdressing and cannot distinguish between one New Look and another, find themselves irresistibly drawn to a scarf. The habit of wearing one came in with the war as a revolt against utility head-wear and bare and dishevelled locks. Designers, or so it strikes an untutored male spectator, drew their inspiration from lamp shades. There was a time when it was possible to see the light through a lamp shade and to read by it, but ingenuity found better ways of hiding the nakedness of the bulb. It came to be encircled and enshrouded by stories told in words or pictures and inviting roving inspection all round the circumference. Attention strays from book and paper in speculations about the fate of the fox that must be somewhere just out of sight round the corner, flying before hounds, or about the next area on the county map. Scarves present problems as inviting and harder to solve, for a lamp shade can be scrutinized in close-up without discourtesy, while the fair stranger on the seat ahead in the bus would properly be affronted if a round, ocular tour of her head and neck was conducted.

Is it the Eiffel Tower or a preview of the South Bank in 1951 peeping out from the folds as they disappear below her coat collar ? Is that a map of Manhattan or of Blackpool ? What are the words of the just indecipherable slogan ? Do they denote loyalty to a football team, or, in the manner of the tattooed arms of sailors, devotion to a named individual ? There is a place for everything, and church is not the place for such questions. Dr. Johnson, a great sabbatarian, said that Sunday should be different, and that people might walk on it, but not throw stones at birds. Casting inquisitive glances at scarves is almost as bad, and, if any old clothes are to be allowed instead of Sunday Best, it will be kinder if pink donkeys are left in the home paddock.

HARRY LAUDER

Two performers stand out above all others in the music-hall. One is DAN LENO, the other HARRY LAUDER, whose death yesterday will sadden many thousands of elderly and middle-aged men and women. Many younger listeners, too, will miss him, for his occasional broadcasts, put on the air until quite recently with all his native verve, made some part of his remarkable personality familiar to those not old enough to have seen him upon the stage. Yet it was only a part that they heard. To understand properly the extraordinary hold which HARRY LAUDER had upon his audience it is necessary to have seen that short, stocky, bandy-legged figure, to know the vitality he put into every movement, to remember the successive looks of jollity, sentiment, and shyness that passed across his face, the twinkle in his eye, the laughter that seemed to make every inch of him shake helplessly. The precision and ease with which he phrased the words as he sang— these were plain to listeners and spectators alike, and they were the expression of a singing technique that seemed as natural as it was accomplished.

When HARRY LAUDER, a young ex-miner from Scotland, first appeared in London in 1900 he reached the music-hall at a moment when it was ripe for change. The old public-house atmosphere was vanishing, and an audience which no longer cared for the more raucous and coarse of the older performers was beginning to look for a different kind of entertainment, certainly not stiff or formal but combining a sense of friendliness and good humour with some sort of subtlety and much better manners. HARRY LAUDER, more than any other, filled the bill. He was, in fact, a new kind of music-hall artist—and not merely because he was the first Scottish comedian to make a really great success in a predominantly Cockney type of entertainment. His charming baritone voice was equally well suited to comic, sentimental and sometimes even solemn songs. In spite of his gift of broad, canny humour—there was his conversation on going to buy a steak at the butcher's—" There you are, sir, tender as a woman's heart." " Thank ye, I'll have sausages "—he was really not primarily a comedian. In such songs as " I love a lassie," " Roamin' in the gloamin'," and a score of others still unforgotten, he was—the word is his own—a minstrel, a singer of ballads for the people. Everywhere, in music-halls or in camps behind the fighting lines, at home or in the Dominions, the people responded by giving him an affection that is not given to many. Few homes will not learn with sadness that HARRY LAUDER has " come to the end of the road."

CURIOUS COLLECTIONS

Among the various self-denials to which a proud centenarian will attribute his staying power, abstention from collecting never appears. He may tell his interviewers that he has been a life-long abstainer from tobacco and alcohol, that the inside of a cinema is as unknown to him as the date of the next election, that the last time he travelled in a train was when Puffing Billy was still on active service and that a visit to London for the Jubilee was the only occasion on which he has slept away from his native village. He never claims to have turned a blind eye on the lure of Blue Mauritius stamps, tram tickets, first editions, great auk's eggs, scarabs, proofs before letters, match-box labels, large copper butterflies and the thousand and one other objects which civilized man (and boy) yearns to gather together as uncontrollably as primitive folk sought to collect cowrie shells or scalps. This silence of the centenarians is significant. The itch to amass something at some stage of life seems to be universal.

Sympathy must, then, be general for the broad-minded collector who, at the age of forty-eight, is reported to have come to the end of his tether. Surrounded by gramophone records and stamps from every country, by cigarette cards and early newspapers going back to the coronation of QUEEN ANNE, he is looking round, baffled, for new worlds to conquer. Specialists, loyal to one branch of this magpie art, will perhaps see in the diversity of their fellow fanatic's plunder the cause of his disenchantment. Had he stuck to cigarette cards he might, they will say, be happily absorbed in arranging and gloating over them and perpetually goading himself with the sight of the blanks. Has he, for instance, every one of those first-class

68

cricketers who passed as currency in the tuck shops and led to blows in the playgrounds of schools of long ago ? Failure to concentrate can, in collecting, as in other ways of passing the time—earning a living included—lead to trouble. Most collectors are uninterested in any hobby except their own. If it is stamps, they will scrutinize another man's album with greedy interest, but, faced by a clutch of rare eggs, only an effort of politeness will persuade them to feign enthusiasm.

Twin charms give collecting its firm hold on the wisest and busiest man no less than on the dilettante. It is irrational and it is not necessarily expensive. Once temptation is fallen for, an outlet may be found to suit any pocket. The millionaire with his scarab is no happier than the lowest income grouper with his tram ticket. When considerations of price or of intrinsic beauty are introduced, the collection instantly loses its pure, amateur status. Rare stamps, as every one who does not collect them knows, are often ugly, smudgy little scraps of paper. First editions are liable to be much less readable than modern cheap editions and, as for manuscripts, it seems to have been a point of honour among some famous authors to cultivate illegible handwriting. Such irrelevancies no more put off a true collector when he has reached years of discretion than grown-up laughter deterred him, at an earlier stage, from spending the afternoon on an embankment, counting trains and logging particulars of their engines. The world, for a collector, is so full of such wonderful things that to-day's victim of satiety will surely turn again like DICK WHITTINGTON.

FULL FATHOM FIVE

" The Admiralty have entered into a contract with the DUKE of ARGYLL to undertake, on a repayment basis, some diving operations in Tobermory Bay, in the Island of Mull, in an attempt to locate a wrecked Spanish galleon alleged to be lying there submerged." Nothing, not even the cautious word " alleged," nor the still more cautious reminder that services must be paid for, can prevent this official statement from making the blood run faster. There are no two words in the English language that carry a richer cargo of history and romance than " Spanish galleon " and when to these are added the slow, cool swing of Tobermory Bay no one would be surprised if the Lords of the Admiralty themselves were to leave their desks in Whitehall and hurry north to the Sound of Mull where the wreck lies beneath the green waters of the Atlantic Ocean.

That there is a wreck has already been proved beyond any doubt. The DUKES of ARGYLL, who possess the right of salvage, have already dragged up from the sea in previous attempts pieces of timber and plate and a bronze cannon which now lies in the grounds of Inveraray Castle, almost as green as the daffodils that grow round it. Local tradition, backed by some historical evidence, believes that it is the Spanish galleon Florencia, one of several known to have been wrecked off this coast when the broken Armada struggled to find its way home in 1588. The story is still told how the ship put in to Tobermory Bay, glad to find shelter after the long voyage and the heavy gales, in order to fill the water-casks. While ashore the Spaniards captured a Highland chief, DONALD GLAS M'LEAN, and took him on board a prisoner. Rather than submit and be taken away to a

70

strange country M'LEAN is said to have found the powder magazine and sunk the ship with all on board.

It is a pretty story and deserves to be a true one. Modern historians, always ready to spoil a good tale, have pointed out that the Florencia returned safely to Spain and modern experts have reduced the possible value of the treasure from a noble figure of £2,000,000 to a miserable £300,000. (If any of it is in gold, however, it should have risen again.) Neither facts nor doubts, however, can dissolve the bronze cannon and the pieces of plate, nor could they chill the hot imagination of ROBERT LOUIS STEVENSON. He must have had the tale in mind when he wrote that fine story " The Merry Men," though he called his galleon the Espirito Santo and sank her in Sandbag Bay and left her " to rot there deep in the sea-tangle and hear the shoutings of the Merry Men as the tide ran high about the island." Perhaps, though the public will wish the DUKE of ARGYLL and the Admiralty well in their brave venture, she is richer there at the bottom of the bay than if she were dredged up and her treasure cleaned of salt and sand and poetry.

UNKIND TO CALORIES

Ringing out clear and pure above the antiphonies of faction, stealing upon our much-borrowed ears as gratefully as the far-off fifes of a relief force, comes the first public utterance of our new MINISTER OF FOOD. " I will try," MR. WEBB has promised, " not to use the word ' calories ' at any time, but just talk about food." Often upon the stage, rather less frequently in what is empirically called real life, we see some quixotic fellow voluntarily sacrifice his superiority over his foe. The sword or the revolver with which he could administer the *coup de grâce* to the cringing villain is summarily cast aside, and this wretch—after a great deal of grunting and the knocking over of several articles of furniture—is finally dispatched with the bare hands (unless it is a historical drama, in which case gauntlets, mailed, may be worn).

A similar impulse of chivalry transfigures the attitude of MR. WEBB. He is quite right in thinking that we are all sick to death of calories, for which we entertain much the same feelings as savages do for the bullets with which they are pacified. But he had no need to renounce the use of this Ministerial ammunition, for it has long since cowed us into submission. To complain about our meagre fare, and still more to contrast it with the succulent and lavish diet of foreigners, was to draw a withering fire to which we had no means of replying. It was wrong, we were told, to suppose that anyone was, or indeed ever had been, better fed than we were. Our calory-intake exceeded that of the average Ruritanian by a handsome margin, and the meals on which our fathers eked out their existence were in the matter of calories much inferior to ours. None doubted the truth of these statistics ; and, although we found them more irritating than persuasive

72

we accepted the calory as a yardstick because it was—
as a bullet is to a savage—invisible, mysterious, and
unanswerable. MR. WEBB could have gone on blazing
away for as long as he liked. But he would not have
increased our love for him.

Although we consume daily innumerable calories, none
of us has ever seen one. Nobody minds the equator (for
instance) being an entirely imaginary line ; the invisibility
of the ampère and the ohm in no way detracts from our
regard for them, and if we were given the chance of
examining under a microscope the germs which we so
freely inhale not all of us, probably, would take it ; but
there is a very widespread feeling that the calory ought to
come out into the open a good deal more than it does if
it is going to hold down its job of being the staff of life.
To popularize it might not at this stage prove easy. It is
unlikely that the election of some more than ordinarily
dazzling female civil servant as Miss Calory, 1950, would
increase to any noticeable extent the gusto with which we
attack our beetroot salad ; nor would the calory make a
very appealing protagonist in a documentary film. The
fact has to be faced that the calory has come to stay ;
but there is no reason why—like some other important
visitors—it should not stay incognito, a state in which
after all it was content to exist during the greater part of
the history of mankind. If MR. WEBB can really manage
to honour his undertaking to " just talk about food " he
will earn our gratitude and respect.

A PLACE FOR EVERYTHING

Everything in its place and a place for everything runs the nursery adage, used by countless generations of nannies in the hope that they may be saved the trouble of tidying up the bricks when their charges have gone to bed. Frequently as the admonition is repeated the world steadfastly refuses to learn the lesson, and household articles still contrive to find themselves anywhere but in the right place, thereby contributing in no small degree to the gaiety of life. Bills become bookmarkers, golf balls lie ignored in porcelain vases, and scissors, to our intense surprise, come to light from the depths of armchairs. In the world outside chaos has also secured a foothold. Old bicycle wheels hang from trees, tin-tacks turn up in cake, and it is not so long since we read of trousers flying from a castle flagstaff. And now a £1 note has won notoriety by appearing in one of the election ballot boxes. The theory that it was deposited there through absent-mindedness is discredited by the information that the note was tightly wrapped in a ballot paper. This was not some harassed mother's shopping money but the result of a deliberate action the exact purpose of which does not spring to mind.

The note may have belonged to an inveterate punter who, familiar with the passing of slips, imagined himself backing his candidate for £1 to win. Bribery, in the hope of persuading the official to count the vote twice, suggests a political fervour foreign to the British temperament. Benevolence is a more probable motive, a fellow-feeling for the teller and a sudden impulse to lighten his burden. Or we may imagine the individual in whom the hoarding instinct is pronounced, and who is unable to face anything resembling a money-box without succumbing to the desire

74

to put something aside for the future. The most likely explanation is simple curiosity, that childish impulse, which survives in all of us, to pull the communication cord and to open the door marked Private, just to " see what would happen." What has happened in this case is that the note has been taken into custody and an opportunity given for it to be claimed. How the *bona fides* of the claimant is to be established we can only guess. Some explanation seems called for and it will require considerable ingenuity to make it sound convincing. Justice, no doubt, will prevail over subterfuge ; or, better still, perhaps the owner, having had his fun, will keep silence, and leave the note to reward the honesty of the finder.

THIS BIJOU

When the house-agent's board goes up nowadays on a London house the adjective used to describe it is a matter of moment. A wrong choice may be most unfortunate. Old-established firms keep a pretty selection of boards, but some of them have entered the category of museum pieces. Pride of place used, for example, to be given to " this magnificent residence ", the sort of place—one exists still in proud desolation—where, among the bell-labels in the basement, was to be found one bearing the inscription " His Lordship's Bathroom." To-day, except perhaps as a potential overflow to a Ministry, the magnificent residence is " out." It is true that there is a London house-agent who, in a local saloon bar when in expansive mood, tells of a mysterious client who bought a magnificent residence with its garage and chauffeur's rooms in the mews behind ; had satanic luck (and the saloon bar narrator means satanic) about licences ; conferred, conspired, and converted ; and two years later emerged triumphant, clutching a profit of just under three hundred pounds on the residence and just over three thousand on the mews cottage, which is now inhabited by a merchant prince. The black arts, however, do not furnish sound general principles for house-dealing.

" Desirable residence " looks well enough, but means little. It might be desirable if one could afford to paint it, to carpet it, and to have it kept clean, but not otherwise. " Non-basement residence " appeals strongly to the housewife, but how rare are the occasions when it can be displayed amid the thousands of acres of Georgian and Victorian London ! Sometimes there is nothing to be done but fall back upon " freehold residence." There is, however, one label with which both the agent and the

76

seller may as a rule feel satisfied. " This bijou residence " suggests a combination of the saleable, the distinguished on that miniature scale which " accords with present-day conditions," and even of the coquettish. It does not imply that there will not be a wilderness of stairs, and it affords no guarantee against a tired heart or dropped arches. It does, however, imply that there will not be long corridors, lofty ceilings, or insoluble problems of space-heating. Above all it is gracious. It hints at a pretty stair-rail, well-proportioned rooms, a nicely panelled drawing-room door. It is not easily bettered in these times. It announces the sort of house a civilized person would like to live in. So at least hopes the prospective vendor awaiting the caller with an order to view, wiping a last thumb-mark off the cream paint and dropping an aspirin into the bowl of flowers so that this bijou may look at its best.

YOUTH AT THE PLOUGH

" Whatever," exclaimed Miss Knibsole on a memorable occasion, " will the young gentlemen be up to next ? " Perhaps the occasion was not really so memorable (for if it was, surely we ought to remember something about it ?). Perhaps the English public have not, until this morning, been afforded an opportunity of familiarizing themselves with the name of Miss Knibsolē, whose character and appearance, accordingly, they are in the strong, the indeed almost god-like, position of being able to delineate and embellish for themselves. Some variation in the relations between literature and life is long overdue ; and the convention whereby commentators on what is new in life may only go for their tags to what is old in literature has never seemed entirely equitable. In life the situations that arise, though they can sometimes fairly be described as " novel " are seldom altogether new ; but in literature, which after all endeavours, however feebly, to make life supportable, a measure of antiquity is *de rigueur* before its aid can be invoked by life's would-be interpreters. This really seems hardly fair ; and he who concocts a new quotation to fit an occurrence cannot be accused of plagiarism or forgery, or indeed of anything worse than an attempt to redress the balance between the old and true in literature and the new and improbable in life.

Besides, the ejaculation attributed to Miss Knibsole expresses so obvious and primordial a sentiment that, if it has not yet found a place in our literature, it is high time that it did. From the minor masterpiece from which anyone who ventured no further than the first sentence of this essay would be justified in believing Miss Knibsole's words to have been taken, her observation is evoked by the news that the Universities of Oxford and Cambridge recently competed in a ploughing match. Whatever, indeed, will the young gentlemen be up to next ? It is true that ploughing has for many decades played an important part in life at both universities and has exerted a decisive effect of the academic career of many a student. But this is a different sort of ploughing ; it is *propter*, not *post hoc* that the homeward plod is apt to begin. It is also true that ploughing in the agricultural sense is a notoriously useful accomplishment. The degree of skill for which it calls is not, however, in these days of such a high order as it was, for—except perhaps on steep hill-sides—the sedentary conduct of a tractor calls for less judgment than the management of even the most habit-ridden horse. But if the ploughman needs less vigilance and gets less exercise than he did, he is given—if the field is long enough—ample opportunities for meditation ; and the urbane traditions of the two universities concerned might well suggest that the mere transformation of stubble or leys into furrow is hardly a worthy test for the competitors who represent them. To convert the whole thing into a bumping race, though it would undoubtedly help to popularize the event, would hardly be consonant with the dignity of agriculture ; but if every ploughman were required, on the completion of his stint, to produce a poem, a thesis or a good thick, raw slice of political philosophy it would dispel for ever the suspicion that these two great seats of learning had sunk to staging contests of a purely utilitarian nature. If the Varsity Ploughing Match is established as a recognized annual event, and if nothing more is required of the contestants than to plough as well (or nearly as well) as an experienced agricultural labourer, it may not be very long before people start getting half-blues for washing up.

DERIVATIONS

"Would you repeat that word?" said the LEADER of the OPPOSITION to the MINISTER of HEALTH. The MINISTER of HEALTH said he would: it was "Goebbelesque," and he proceeded to explain its meaning, which was not, as might have been expected, a very pretty one. The word itself does not seem a very pretty one either, nor easy to enunciate. If some spluttering orator were in the heat of the moment to accuse his adversary of grotesque Goebbelesqueries, he might get himself into a verbal tangle worthy of Peter Piper or Sister Susie. And yet it is hard to say whether MR. BEVAN could have done much better. Goebbelian, Goebbeleian, Goebbelistic, Goebbelite, or Goebbels-like—none of these is really attractive nor flows trippingly off the tongue. Perhaps if the root is rotten no flower of language can prosper. However there is still one further depth possible. Supposing it to be within the limits of parliamentary decorum, one right honourable gentleman might call another a Goebbellard. This, as many will remember, was the termination which so infuriated the Arabian author of *The Dynamiter* that he broke out into a long passage in too Oriental a style. "Any writard," he said, "who writes dynamitard shall find in me a never-resting fightard." Yet, in spite of this splendid defiance the word "dynamitard" is still regrettably to be found in the dictionary.

These derivatives are constantly giving trouble. Many nouns are so awkward and obstinate that it is utterly impossible to extract from them a decently sounding adjective. Try one termination after another and no one of them fits. This is specially noticeable in the titles given to the old boys of various schools. Some run easily and

80

smoothly enough, such as Rugbeians or Etonians; the Carthusians have had a beautiful and legitimate alternative ready to their hands. But there are illustrious names that do not easily produce manageable adjectives and then the name of the pious founder must be prayed in aid. Wykehamists and Alleynians are certainly more pleasing to the ear than Winchesterians and Dulwichians. For that matter Oxfordians and Cambridgians would never do. Luckily they can both be helped out, though not with equal success, by the Latin. Among Scottish schools there are some with names presumably so tongue-twisting that they are reduced to the letters F.P. standing for "Former Pupils." This has a prosaic sound, not likely to generate patriotic enthusiasm. Yet Scotland has one such title with which England cannot hope to compete. How nobly sonorous are the Fettesian-Lorettonians. Generally speaking there are numberless Old Some-thingians, but no single example of Old Somethingesques. Here is a chance for some academy to distinguish itself.

F

THE SCHOOLBOYS' HOLMES

People are apt to complain that some classical author, such as SCOTT or DICKENS, has been permanently spoilt for them, since they were compelled to read him in youth, and sometimes—to add insult to injury—to read him with notes and a glossary. It may be said that he who could never look at *Ivanhoe* or *Pickwick* again on that account must be but a poor creature who would anyhow have come to a bad end. Still, the complaint is heard so often that it cannot be wholly neglected, and it must be granted that notes which are gratefully received when giving a clue to construing Latin or Greek are merely a bore when they explain that Muggleton may possibly be Maidstone or Eatanswill Sunbury. Rightly or wrongly, another classic has now been submitted to this process and there have been published three Sherlock Holmes readers, if they may so be termed, each containing three of the stories and each story followed by a notes and questions. Here is no cause for alarm. The notes for the most part only simplify what the juvenile student would call " long words," though here and there they are more exciting, as when in *Silver Blaze* they explain to the innocent in racing matters the meaning of the price growing shorter and shorter and define " touts " as " a vulgar word for men who hang round racing stables and racecourses." If incidentally the notemaker could have enumerated all the acts in that story for which someone must infallibly have been warned off the turf, he would have done good service to serious grown-up study, but wisely no doubt he did not want to put things into the child's head.

Most people will probably think he is right and that the boy reader of Sherlock Holmes should be, in his early

82

stages at any rate, a fundamentalist, having an utter and simple faith in the sacred writing. There is no reason, they will say, why he should not deduce that Holmes was at Cambridge from the singular incident of Victor Trevor's bull-terrier. That is a justifiable and entirely pious piece of research, by all means to be encouraged. On the other hand, there is something almost blasphemous in asserting that Professor Moriarty cannot have been trying to murder Mr. Douglas in Sussex in 1899 because he had tumbled into the Reichenbach falls in 1891. *Procul, O procul este profani!* The book says he did and that suffices. When the boy grows older, old enough to think for himself, he may, if he likes, take to these sacrilegious antics, which often compel admiration by their intellectual brilliancy while they shock by their impiety. It would be idle to deny that those who indulge in them are eminent and learned persons, but it is open to question whether they are as happy as the poor, stupid fundamentalist re-reading the stories for the fiftieth time with never the ghost of a doubt. If then, as many will hope, the boy accepts the stories, at least to begin with, quite literally, he will find not a word in these slender little volumes to corrupt him. It is pleasant to think of him setting out on this joyous adventure on the long, long trail from the Scandal in Bohemia to the Retired Colourman.

WATCH THIS SPACE

An access of self-importance (which has often in the past proved for one reason or another transitory) sometimes leads foreign countries to claim that they invented almost everything worth inventing. This harmless and even engaging form of megalomania has lately attacked the Russians. To them, they have in recent months asserted, the world owes the steam-engine, penicillin, jet-propelled aircraft, the planets Mars and Venus, dynamite, radar, and the horse-drawn railroad, to say nothing of anaesthesia, the adding machine and countless other of the amenities which make modern life supportable. We have our own biased and distorted views as to where some of these things originated ; but we do not trouble to advance them—except perhaps in the case of the horse-drawn railroad, which is the sort of thing people are rather apt to feel strongly about and which no true Briton believes to have made its first appearance on this planet earlier than that ever-memorable September 27, 1825, when the metals of the Stockton and Darlington railway reverberated to its passage. As for penicillin and radar and the rest, " Have it," experience has taught us to murmur, " your own way."

So ingrained in the Soviet mind had appeared this habit of claiming primacy in all fields of human endeavour that it is with something of a shock that we find a Vice-Premier of the U.S.S.R saying, as MR. MIKOYAN did the other day : " It is time to think seriously of the organization of advertising." He continued in terms which made it clear that Russia does not, at any rate for the present, regard herself as having invented advertising. " We do not aspire," said MR. MIKOYAN, " to overtake the capitalist countries in this field, because with them advertising is a means of shamelessly deceiving the consumer. We must develop our Soviet advertising, which will be cultural and progressive." Having got over our surprise at discovering that a nation which invented jet-propelled aircraft as long ago as 1899 has only just got around to realizing that it pays to advertise, we can hardly help speculating about the lines on which this practice will develop in Russia. That those lines will be progressive and cultural almost went without saying : and the character of the Soviet régime is such that we can rest assured that what appears in the advertisements will be absolutely true. But how exactly will it work ? All means of production and distribution, as well as all trading organizations, are owned and run by the State ; and this fact, combined with the need for absolute veracity, is likely to produce a tradition of advertising so novel that it will soon put the Russians in a position to assert that they invented the whole racket, anyhow. There will be a sober, objective tone, an absence of hyperbole. Sovbagshot (if that is the organization concerned) will not advertise " The Perfect Samovar " but rather " The Best Samovar which Socialist Industry in its Present Stage of Development has been Able to Produce." The traveller will not find the streets of Tiflis or Tashkent placarded, by Narkatnip, with posters declaring " All the Best People wear Bedsocks " or " When in Doubt, Light a February the Sixteenth ! " ; such statements would imply in their governmental sponsors a tendency to bourgeois snobbery as well as a deviationist tolerance of doubt. It looks, in fact, as if the Russians had set themselves a rather delicate problem. They will doubtless approach it cautiously, learning wherever they can from other countries whose Governments have gone into the advertising business in a big way. Our own, though it seems to have little flair in this direction, can offer at least one small but practical hint. The People's Commissariats of Internal Affairs and State Security can make a confident start by copying our own Ministry of Transport in one of its better known publicity campaigns ; for Russia is one of those modern democracies in which posters warning the populace to " Mind How You Go " would have a message for every one.

MOUSTACHE-CONTROL

A native of Jutland is under pressure from the Danish police to reduce the dimensions of his moustache. This luxuriant growth is of the handle-bar type. The police want it reduced to toothbrush size, because they think this might help them to identify the perpetrator of certain offences committed at a time when, as it happens, this particular moustache was much smaller than it is to-day. The whole matter being *sub judice* (and likely, at a guess, to remain so until the Human Rights Commission of the United Nations have given their ruling on the whole principle of *habeas fungus*), any comment would be improper. But it does serve to remind us of the uncertainties and even dangers which must ultimately arise in any country (and Great Britain, alas, is such a one) where a tradition of *laissez-faire* is allowed to permeate the community's attitude to moustaches.

The decision to grow a moustache can be compared with the decision to get married, except that the number of ladies who have carried out both decisions must be much smaller than the number of gentlemen. Few if any of us are born with moustaches, and to cultivate one is to effect at least a semi-permanent alteration in the appearance and may possibly lead to modification or development of the character. Yet this step—far more momentous than many other forms of private enterprise which are now subject to the paternal control of the State—is left entirely to our own discretion. If we acquire a puppy we have to take out a dog licence, if we wish to build a pigsty we must first get permission from the Minister of Town and Country Planning, and if we wish to kill a pig his colleague of Agriculture and Fisheries must sanction the dread but short-lived enterprise. A wife, a wireless set, a week-end

87

in Paris, the felling of a tree or the purchase of a rook-rifle—none of these can be undertaken until the State has issued the necessary licence, permit, or certificate. In order to erect a summer-house in our garden, where it will be invisible to all eyes save our own, we must submit quadruplicate applications to the authorities ; yet we can encourage at will upon our face strange hirsute growths calculated in many cases to repel or to intimidate the world at large. Such tolerance, so gross a negation of planning values, is but one remove from anarchy.

Even in the services, where formerly moustaches were the subject of rigid disciplinary enactments, control is slipping. The Army has never been the same since, in 1916, our gallant lads were told that they might shave their upper lips ; and this once proudly and compulsorily bristling feature is now not even mentioned in the relevant sub-paragraph of King's Regulations, which ends, on a note of plaintive imprecision, " Whiskers, if worn, will be of a moderate length." The Navy takes a firmer stand, though our respect for its implied abhorrence of moustaches would be greater if it were expressed in manlier, more forthright terms, for King's Regulations, after empowering the captain of a ship to permit his crew " to wear beards and moustaches if they so desire," proceed with almost Oriental cunning to lay down that by those who do so desire " the use of the razor is to be discontinued entirely, as moustaches are not to be worn without the beard or the beard without moustaches." Nothing better illustrates the woful confusion surrounding the whole question of moustaches than the fact that a conscientious citizen who cannot decide whether to grow one or not can only resolve this personal problem by enlisting in the Royal Navy ; and it is high time that this chink in the cotton wool with which the welfare State surrounds us was blocked, once and for ever, by some more than ordinarily ridiculous piece of legislation.

MICE IN VOGUE

The latest Paris fashions, a periodical devoted to such matters informs us, " begin and end on the premise of ' no camouflage ' " and just for a moment we entertain the illusion that the ladies will be looking less ridiculous this year. But a couple of paragraphs later on we find ourselves reading " Apron skirts with the apron wrapping either from front to back or from back to front do not necessarily break the strictly straight skirt line " ; and " even the lower waist-lines manage to be both low *and* normal by means of a low hipband beginning at the normal waist-line." So that it sounds as if, in the modiste's motto for 1950, either the word " camouflage " or the word " no " has some meaning other than those normally attributed to them. It is accordingly with a sensation of relief that, disengaging ourselves from the convolutions of a prose style so (as its practitioners might say) exigently *insaisissable*, we learn that a lady has been seen walking in Fifth Avenue with a live mouse in her hat. The tiny rodent was imprisoned in what is described as a pill-box of transparent plastic and was clearly visible to the passers-by, whom it, for its part, was in a good position to quiz as it travelled impressively through their midst like a very small maharajah on a very large elephant.

Most men will feel for this lady a warm impulse of admiration and affection. If we chanced to sit next to her at luncheon, how much less onerous than usual should we find the task of making polite conversation. The dullest boor, the shyest oaf, would never be at a loss for something to say.. On stage and screen a little child used often to be depicted as drawing an estranged couple together. The mouse would play a roughly similar role—

89

except, of course, that there would never be the slightest risk of our being estranged. Fascinating though we should find her answers to our questions, she would be scarcely less interested in the information which we should be in a position to give her. In its little conning-tower her darling would be invisible to its owner and she would turn appealingly to us for a ringside commentary on his doings. "He's coming out of his corner. . . . He's down ! . . . No, he's up again. . . . What beautiful footwork ! . . . He's still looking a bit shaken ; I don't think he's quite recovered from your last sneeze. . . ." It could never be said of a woman with a mouse in her hat that she was difficult to talk to.

Whether the pioneer from New York will be equally popular with her own sex is doubtful. Between ladies and mice there has always been a certain coldness, and the close family resemblance between these little furry friends is a further drawback, for no lady of fashion likes, on arriving at a party, to find that two or three of her rivals are wearing to all intents and purposes the same rodent that she is. There is, however, no reason why the mode should stop short at mice. There are many other forms of livestock which can be carried on the head of even the most ethereal beauty. Lizards, frogs, moles, and slow-worms—to name only a few—are all eminently portable ; and though the glossy pages of the fashion magazines have not yet carried an illustration with the caption " Importantly enhancing the challenge of So-and-So's latest model is this crisply masculine stag-beetle," the day may not be far distant when we shall be treated to something equally nonsensical.

THE CLUB BORE

It is not a hush, it is not even a sharp intake of breath that greets his appearance in our midst ; yet momentarily there is a sort of shudder in the conversation, as though a catspaw, precursor to a storm, had skimmed athwart the ripples of our talk. Were he a rogue elephant (and his unperspicuous yet determined eyes almost warrant the analogy) and we so many pygmies in a jungle clearing, we should all instantly climb up trees, uttering shrill cries of alarm. But you cannot do that sort of thing in a London club ; there are not the facilities for it and it is in any case not in the tradition. Terror clutches at our hearts ; yet, like French aristocrats in a communal dungeon, we preserve an impassive and disinterested mien. Someone is for it ; heaven send it be not us.

Here and there, it is true, a slight shuffling of feet, a cautious scraping of chair-legs on the carpet make themselves heard as each little knot of gossips or pontificants closes its ranks, like a covey of partridges huddling together on a frosty evening. Isolated members sit down with wary expedition at any writing tables that are vacant and proceed, with heads bowed and shoulders hunched protectively, to write unexpected letters to their godchildren. One or two poor wretches, too inexperienced to apprehend the dangers of doing so, take cover behind evening papers, thus giving him whose company they shun an easy chance of making contact by offering a comment upon, or making an inquiry about, the events of the day. In an armchair by the fire a very old member adopts with his usual sagacity the well-tried expedient of feigning death.

Only he is safe. No matter how serried the phalanx of our backs, no matter how clearly our lowered voices

91

indicate the private nature of our conversation, the club bore will get his oar in if he wants to. He makes his own cues. He finds it extraordinary that we should be talking about Smith, for he ran into Smith's sister-in-law at Harrogate last year—no, it was the year before. She, of course, was a Jones. And off he goes, swinging from one family tree to another like a great baboon, airing as he goes his grievances against society, propounding his remedies for the nation's ills, driving the steam-roller of his reminiscences over us with a terrible deliberation. There is a certain morbid fascination in watching him, mouthing so (one must presume) happily away. Why do we let him do this to us ? In the distant days when we were all savages, in the slightly less distant days when we were boys, the community knew how to protect itself against this sort of thing. Why does nobody fell him with the poker, or even tell him to shut up ? But generally our extremist impulse is short-lived. We remember that it is a law of nature that every club must have its bore. This one (who like all his kind is miraculously, inexplicably unaware of his status) will not last for ever ; and who knows but what we ourselves, in the years to come, may not be destined to succeed him ?

THE FACTS OF LIFE

To see ourselves as others see us is supposed, like having a cold bath in the morning, to be salutary ; to see ourselves as statisticians see us is an experience whose benefits are often abstruse. In a recent publication which anatomizes in some detail the tastes and habits of our island community, the statisticians have a whale of a time. Now zigzag, now undulant, their graphs record our joint peculiarities with lapidary finality. Three graceful lines, sweeping downwards like a drawing of a horse's tail by an inferior Chinese artist, chart the " percentage of women in each social class using lipstick in any one week, analysed by age." We note with interest that, although females of the upper class start applying the stuff later in life than their ex-inferiors, they make up for this by going on using it a good deal longer, no less than 20 per cent. being still at it when they reach seventy. The only possible criticism of this interesting graph is that to leave it unaccompanied by a similar diagram showing what proportion of women tint the nether lip before the upper, and vice versa, savours of the superficial.

Nothing, on the other hand, can be said against the bold, assured manner in which the " numbers and proportions of the ' adult ' population actually on holiday away from home at any particular time during the holiday months " is depicted. This graph (to whose other attractions must be added the fact that if it were torn from its context it could with the help of water-colours be converted into a picture of Mount Fujiyama) consists only of a single line, rising steadily from the beginning of June to the beginning of August and thereafter not less steadily descending. Its conclusions are inescapable ; here is proof, if proof were needed, that the height of the holiday season is the height of the holiday season.

Another hand, one rather imagines, was engaged on some of the more *pointilliste* canvasses ; on, for instance, the calculations which show that during the first quarter of 1949 each cage-bird-owning family at the top of the social scale owned ·28 of a cage-bird less than its proletarian counterpart. Impersonal and objective though the tone of all these inquiries is, a note of bias does creep in here and there. There is, for instance, a touch of asperity—the relic, perhaps, of some embittering personal experience—in the section dealing with " numbers and proportions of women who have permanent waves at all, and numbers and proportions doing so in any one month —first quarter, 1949." The 19,830,000 heroines of this chapter are classified as :—

Housewives—non-working	11,040,000
Housewives—working	3,720,000
Other women	5,070,000

To tell 11,040,000 housewives that they are non-working is a bold thing to do ; and to enhance the ever-present menace of the Other Woman by revealing that, apart from everything else, she has a big numerical superiority over the working housewife was hardly kind to that poor, loyal drudge. But, for all that, this is a remarkable compilation ; and if it goes into a second edition many of its readers will hope that the statisticians will allow themselves to be a little more subjective, to tell us something about themselves. In their own way, of course. A short appendix on " numbers and proportions of statisticians who care a brass farthing how many citizens of sixty-five and over used a bicycle once a week or less frequently during the first quarter of 1949 " might produce a very cute little graph.

ORDER IN COURT

It is pleasant for the man whose life is not packed with excitement to imagine what his reactions would be in face of the unexpected. What would he do, he asks himself, if his clothes were stolen while he was bathing ; how would he behave if he found a burglar under his bed or a Cabinet Minister occupying his seat at the theatre ? The heroes of light literature leave him in no doubt what his conduct ought to be. An imperceptible setting of the jaw, a narrowing of the eyes, perhaps a sharp intake of breath—these are the only signs of emotion permitted as the trained mind formulates a plan of action behind an otherwise impassive countenance. Sometimes from the depths of his armchair the dreamer may identify himself with the cool man of action ; more often he will admit his own shortcomings and reflect that if ever he is put to the test he will be lucky to muddle through without making a fool of himself.

A recent incident at Penzance county court, in which the hair of a witness was observed by the registrar to be alight, is a reminder that man's mastery of the unexpected is not confined to the realm of fiction. Law courts are a stage on which are paraded many human idiosyncrasies, and registrars will be familiar with individuals who twitch or tremble or roll their eyes, as well as with those who mop their brows or stand on one foot ; but they might well be expected to display alarm on being confronted by a man with smoke pouring from his head. In this particular instance the registrar approached the matter, if we may judge from the bare facts of the case, in a discreet and unruffled manner. His question, " Are you smoking ? ", while hinting at the nature of the conversation to come, paid due regard to the proprieties of the court. The preliminary skirmish having been answered in the negative there followed the conclusion delivered in unemotional monosyllables : " Well, then, your head is on fire." This discouraging information was apparently received in the witness-box with a sang-froid in keeping with the high standard already set. The outbreak —which had been started by some inflammatory substance dropping from a gas bracket on to the hair of the witness— was quickly brought under control and the submission of evidence continued. The onlooker—from his armchair— will applaud the performance, and secretly hope that the next time he drops a lighted match into the waste-paper basket he may resolve the situation as simply and with as little loss of dignity.

VALEDICTION FOR SOUP

One of the minor disadvantages about passing from the darker half-year to the brighter is that one must bid temporary farewell to a real thick soup. Though the small preliminary bowlfuls which appear in restaurants and at banquets will continue to be served and are well-meaning appetizers, only in domestic soup is the true quality of greatness apprehended. " It is the nature of all greatness not to be exact," BURKE tells us ; and certainly there should be nothing exact, in quantity, definition or consistency about the finest specimens of soup that in winter rejoice the home. Every self-respecting family has no doubt its own tradition in this vital matter. Those who plume themselves upon a rarefied taste may write him down a vulgarian who looks with misgiving on the julienne ; yet the denser the mixture the more exciting, and when it comes thick and slab, so that the ladle stands almost upright, when one knows that the piping tureen is not being drained to supply one plateful apiece but is ardent with desire to disgorge its further riches, soup surely has the value of half a meal. It surpasses alike the dish of herbs and the stalled ox. It is taken in perfection at the kitchen fireside after a hot bath late at night.

The cauldron of the secret, black, and midnight hags ; the conglomeration of delicacies which newspapers sometimes relate as found in the stomach of an ostrich ; the fierce ingredients of the White Knight's pudding, which began with blotting paper ; all these but palter at mixtures in comparison with the ideal soup. In colour it should suggest a sea suffused by all the dyes of the ocean. Amid isles of potato and submerged reefs of barley will be cruising chopped carrot, scooped onion, convoys of peas—a whole navy in the gravy, to transform the line in BETTE

97

DAVIS'S song. To take bread separately is gross insult to an honest broth, which contains in itself the stay as well as the juice of sustenance. Soup trains the virtue of restraint, for the greedy burn their tongues. It affords puzzles in ingenuity if splash and noise are to be avoided. It sharpens the discrimination of the palate in detecting various flavours ; while any novice may be certain about the tomato, expert attention and long experience are needed to notice the celery. Neither food nor drink, soup partakes of and is above both ; thus bearing out the philosophic contention that truths contained in apparent opposites are reconciled in a higher unity. Considered as a term in philosophy, soup is perhaps the Formal Cause of ARISTOTLE, the Absolute of HEGEL, or the Life Force of BERGSON ; the alkahest, the elixir, the quintessence. It is also readily digestible, which those conceptions sometimes are not.

A BIT OF PLAY ACTING

A learned judge lately asked the jury to consider whether a bit of play acting would do any harm to anybody. In the particular case the jury clearly thought it would not, but the question can have a wider application. Leaving the audience out of the argument, play acting can cause exquisite agony to some who take part. No sympathy is needed by those who, like Bottom, first and greatest of the amateurs, believe themselves capable of Pyramus, Thisbe and the lion all at once, but there is nearly always some pathetic creature dragged in most unwillingly by the heels to play a minor character. There was once a dear old gentleman who as a docile subaltern had been forced to take part in some regimental theatricals. For the rest of his long life he kept a tattered cutting from a local paper, as a warning to anyone who should try to tempt him again to tread the boards. " Mr. So-and-so," thus ran the passage, " bears an honoured name but he will pardon us for saying that he is not a delineator of character." There have been others, to whom the criticism would have been equally applicable, less appreciative of their own limitations. Fortunately most of us are of the same opinion as was poor little Fanny Price when she was pressed to play the cottager's wife in the theatricals at Mansfield Park. " Me ! " she cried, " Indeed you must excuse me. I could not act anything if you were to give me the world."

That particular performance of *Lovers' Vows* came, it will be remembered, to a sad end. After Edmund had at first objected on grounds of decorum and then given way, after Mr. Rushworth had wondered whether he would know himself in a blue dress and a pink satin cloak, after the bookshelf had been moved and twenty pounds or so spent on a little carpenter's work and a green curtain, Sir Thomas Bertram put an end to it all by returning prematurely from the West Indies. Yet the preparations had occupied six whole delightful chapters for which we are eternally grateful, and indeed it seems that literature was once much fuller of private theatricals than it is to-day. Private theatricals ! The very name seems to have about it something of an elder fashion. There was, for example, that grand entertainment at Lord Steyne's when Becky played Clytemnestra and the little French Marquise, at once the consummation of her triumphs and the beginning of her downfall. Descend to a humbler but still pleasant walk of life, Frank Fairleigh, and there is the charade they acted at Heathfield set out at full length. Moreover, at a later date, DU MAURIER's enchanting drawings in *Punch* are full of ladies in powder and patches and the ambitious couple who mean to give *The Cup* in their back drawing-room. It would almost seem that now the times are too hard and too busy and the paraphernalia too expensive. There are, of course, more numerous than ever, the immensely serious and skilful amateur performances, played almost professionally on a proper stage ; but a bit of play acting is now only an amusement for the nursery on a wet day.

THINKS

" A penny for your thoughts." It was not a very handsome offer, but at least it showed that someone was interested in what was going on inside our head. It might have been supposed that this interest would have become keener and more marked as we grew older. Fascinating though the products of our mental processes were in early youth, the curious and powerful organism responsible for them ought surely to have gained, with maturity, an irresistible allure. Yet before we are half way through the first of the several decades which make up that protracted period known as the prime of life we begin to notice that people have stopped offering us a penny for our thoughts. This is not because, out of respect for our now massive intellects, they have raised the ante. They do not bid a florin or a guinea ; they do not bid at all. The mystery which seemed so well worth probing to our favourite aunt or to the pretty girl in pink with whom we sat out the Charleston at the local hunt ball has lost its power to intrigue. We still, at times, look pensive ; we even occasionally think. But people no longer say to us, rather archly : " A penny for your thoughts."

The effect upon our self-esteem is, of course, as negligible as the effect upon our exchequer ; but it is rather odd, all the same. Our thoughts may in fact be very boring thoughts, but not everybody knows that this is so. Frequenters of the esplanade may know better than to waste a penny on " What the Butler Saw," but there must surely be simple-minded strangers who would like—or who think they would like—a peep into our minds. If they took one, they might be repelled by the disorder, for there is no doubt that most of our minds grow increasingly untidy. Our thoughts are neither so explicit nor so easily decipherable as the thoughts which emerge so appositely, in floating white bubbles, from the crania of the *dramatis personae* in advertisements and strip cartoons. "*THINKS:*" (we read in one of these vaguely ectoplasmic emanations) "*I am losing my grip. I don't seem able to concentrate*"; and our heart goes out to the bowed, haggard figure from whose left ear this grim diagnosis appears to have materialized.

Our compassion is sometimes qualified with envy. There are moments when we, too, find it difficult to concentrate, when it is hard to resist the conclusion that we are losing our grip, when anyone who offered a penny for our thoughts would get the cerebral equivalent of a dog's breakfast. But these crises would be easily supportable if we could analyse them as succinctly as do the originators of these aerial asides. If we suddenly found ourselves tethered to a bubble, twice the size of our own head, with "*THINKS: I am losing my grip*" printed on it in block capitals we should very quickly either clarify our mind or withdraw from society. The idea of having our innermost thoughts displayed on a sort of airborne pumpkin hovering over our heads is not, however, one that makes a very strong appeal to the British. A certain amount of mind-reading is all very well in its way, but all thinking people will agree that most thoughts are best kept under the hat.

THE RIVALS

The goddess who presides over the draw, decreeing how the names shall come out of the hat, is doubtless a lady upon whose honour no aspersions are permissible. And yet it is sometimes hard not to believe that she takes an impish pleasure in robbing us, as she has lately done, of a historic encounter. " Have ye music ? " said Alan Breck. " I can pipe like a Macrimmon," cried Robin Oig. " And that is a very bold word," answered Alan. It was touch and go between the pipes and the sword, and many people had been hoping that something like that noble scene might be re-enacted not in Balquidder but at St. Andrews, not with music but with golf clubs. Those two redoubtable vocalists MR. BING CROSBY and MR. DONALD PEERS have entered for the Amateur Championship which falls to be played there next week. What a clash it would have been if that goddess had given her kindly aid, but she capriciously decided that the two should be so far apart in the draw that, so statisticians aver, they cannot meet until the final, and that with all possible respect for both gentlemen makes it comparatively unlikely that they will meet at all.

This is to be sad news for the armies of their respective fans, but it is an ill wind that blows nobody good, and the stewards who have to control these enthusiasts will be far from unhappy. At St. Andrews to-day the spectators are herded right off the course among the whins, so that the players pursue their way in a strange, almost uncanny, solitude, watched only from a distance. This plan has worked admirably hitherto, but discipline has its limits, and it might have been that hundreds of maddened ladies would suddenly have defied the rope and swooped upon their victims. So if those two great names had come out together some hard-driven committeeman might have been moved to tamper with his honour, put one of them back and take a fresh dip into the lucky bag. There has, however, been no such dreadful temptation, for each hero has at least half one day all to himself; MR. CROSBY sets out before 10 o'clock on Monday morning and MR. PEERS not till nearly 3 in the afternoon. There will be just time to recover in between.

DADDY'S BUSY

To the world at large few professions seem more delightful than that of literature. Its technique is so simple, the capital equipment required so inexpensive and so portable, the routine so elastic. No trains to catch, no clocks to punch, no one to call " Sir "—it is small wonder that the writer is often told (in a phrase which he sometimes feels might have been more happily chosen) that he is a lucky beggar. He rather resents this envy ; and, though he does not exactly return it, there are moments when he almost wishes that he himself were only a cog instead of being the whole of an unreliable and obsolescent machine. How reassuring to enter the stately block of offices, already made shipshape by cohorts of charwomen and manned by lift-men, secretaries, and telephone operators ! A trim engagement pad warns him of the conferences he must attend ; he will lunch economically in the canteen ; perhaps in the afternoon he will run down to the new factory in one of the office cars. And if by mischance in the course of these activities he should suddenly expire, they will say that he died in harness.

In harness. . . . It is for lack of these metaphorical trappings that the writer sometimes feels forlorn. He does not particularly want to attend one of the conferences which (he vaguely understands) so frequently engage the energies of business executives, but it would be nice if he could occasionally say—or rather if his secretary could say—that he was attending one. To be closeted with your Muse is, no doubt, better than to be closeted with your managing director, but it does not give the same degree of security from interruption ; and the process—difficult and delicate though it is—of changing a typewriter ribbon has not about it the pioneering glamour, the technical *mystique*, associated—at any rate in the minds of those who know no better—with a visit to a new factory.

Prominent among those who know no better are the writer's children. Their puny intellects seem incapable of grasping the fact that their father, while seated in a disconsolate attitude and gazing vacantly out of the window, is in fact pursuing an arduous and exacting profession. " Go away," cries the poor wretch ; " Daddy's busy." The children come a little closer. " But what are you doing ? " they ask ; and his Muse decamps on one of her innumerable afternoons off. How can the little idiots be made to see the connexion, the stern and important connexion, between the virgin foolscap on their father's desk and the bread and butter which they consume with such an extraordinarily bad grace at tea ? How explain to them the things they need to know about that Muse—her neurotic aversion to all forms of noise, her complete lack of interest in the eggs of the chaffinch, her Snark-like capacity for softly and silently fading away. Oh, for the calculating machines, the conveyor-belts, the glass doors marked " Inquiries," the steel doors marked " Research," entrenched behind which more fortunate parents win bread for their loved ones ! Their tasks may be humdrum or even sordid, they may have to work on Saturday mornings ; but at least their lifework is not periodically thrown out of gear, at least they are not at intervals obliged to bleat, in accents half minatory, half wheedling, and wholly disregarded, " Daddy's busy. Go away."

DON FLIES FROM QUAD

Some were pleased, some were shocked, none remained indifferent on hearing that the VICE-CHANCELLOR of OXFORD UNIVERSITY, accompanied by his spouse, is to take off to-morrow from one of the quadrangles of Christ Church in a helicopter, thus incidentally presenting the PUBLIC ORATOR with the equivalent of a half-volley outside the leg stump. The purpose of DR. LOWE's ascent is severely practical, for only by adopting this means of transport can he sandwich in between his other engagements a banquet in far-off Torquay, where he is to be the guest of honour of the Master Printers' Federation. Peckwater and Tom have seen plenty of unusual sights in their time ; but hitherto there has been an unbroken tendency for the laws of gravity, when challenged or even trifled with, to assert themselves successfully. Between their ancient walls many have fallen, for one reason or another, to the ground ; none, till now, has risen from it into the air.

While there will be general regret that the VICE-CHANCELLOR was unable to take passage in a balloon—an engine whose out-of-date appearance and feckless method of progression would really have been more in keeping with the Oxford tradition—a helicopter ought not to prove unacceptable to the *genius loci*. Although it is very modern, it looks rather antiquated ; and as it rises slowly but noisily past the window-boxes, whirling its arms madly like a Continental policeman on traffic duty, and gains the upper air it will seem a pleasantly fantastic anachronism among the dreaming spires. The master printers are to be congratulated on organizing this air-lift.

107

There are, however, those who will feel that a precedent of some danger has been established. At present there are not many helicopters about, but soon there will be more ; and in the end these machines may come to play a baleful part in the lives of the eminent. No longer will the letters inviting them to lecture, to give away prizes, to open fêtes, to lay foundation-stones end with a paragraph about the train service. No longer will their replies offer, amid a shower of crocodile tears, a *non possumus* based on considerations of time and space. Every head mistress will have her helicopter, and the honorary secretaries of literary societies will be accustomed to pick up celebrities as a hovering kestrel picks up fieldmice. It is a bleak outlook for those famous people in whom the sound of their own voices, struggling with the acoustics of the Corn Exchange or buffeted by the flapping of a marquee, awakens only dejection and self-disgust ; and in these quarters there is a strong disposition to feel that the Home of Lost Causes has sold the pass.

PERSONAL APPEARANCE

At a recent meeting of Equity, we read, " a young actor in spectacles, with an academic air and immaculately pressed suit, was violently cheered by actor-colleagues when he called upon them to chain themselves to street-railings to focus public attention on the British film crisis." It is, one must admit, a stupendous idea. Members of the public, who find it difficult to focus their attention on any crisis for more than two minutes at a time, will wait with some eagerness to see it put into practice. The opportunity to see Dame So-and-So or Sir John Such-and-Such spreadeagled on the rails of one of our better-known squares is one which can hardly be expected to recur very often and should certainly not be missed by any student of the modern theatre. Even the least film-minded of us might be able to focus his attention for, say, half an hour, if stimulated by the spectacle—and no other word is conceivable—of the chorus at Drury Lane padlocked at intervals to the lamp-posts of Piccadilly. Those of us who are fortunate enough still to possess railings of our own would gladly offer them, free of charge, as a suitable stance for a retired Shakespearian actor who would be expected in return to declaim passages from *Prometheus Bound* to the passers by.

It is to be feared, however, that certain difficulties might arise in practice. Clearly some railings would be considered more *chic* than others and awkward questions of precedence might arise. There are, unfortunately, conspicuously few railings of any kind in Shaftesbury Avenue, so that actors and actresses would be forced to go a little farther afield than is usual. The gates of Buckingham Palace would be showy, if a trifle " ham." The former gates of Devonshire House in the Green Park would

109

form a decorative background for any actress, but might lead people to think that she was merely posing for some more than usually lunatic photograph in a fashion magazine. The railings round the Houses of Parliament would probably be best, but even so there would be a risk of some confusion with the latest Communist peace demonstration or, worse still, of bringing out the CHANCELLOR of the EXCHEQUER to collect entertainment tax.

There is also the question of time. No doubt members of the profession, which is not unskilled in matters of publicity, would advertise their appearance beforehand, but how long would they wait? One can imagine anxious managers touring round London with a hacksaw in order to release their charges in time for the *matinée* at 2.30. Who would be given the key? As the originator of the whole scheme the " young actor in spectacles with an academic air and immaculately pressed suit " would have some claim to the part of first gaoler, but an ugly situation might arise if it were discovered that, carried away by his enthusiasm, he had chained himself to some modest railing and thrown the key into the river. In addition to a film crisis we should then quickly have a crisis in the theatre. The more closely the plan is considered the less practicable it appears. We modestly suggest an alternative for the consideration of Equity. Instead of chaining actors to street-railings, they might chain theatre-goers to their seats. Nothing would make a more lasting impression than that.

ANYTHING TO DECLARE

Honesty is relative, and many a man and woman who would blush if one of their cheques were " returned to drawer " will make timid little raids across the frontier of strict rectitude. Now that the Whitsun crowds are swarming up the gangways at the Channel ports these must be a trial to the Customs men, who belong to that large class of public servants which deserves more sympathy than it gets. Sea traffic keeps awkward hours, but those uniformed figures, looking like a cross between a naval and a merchant marine officer, are always ready behind their long wooden counters to trap contraband. They know full well, unless they are less astute than their grave and sometimes rather inquisitorial faces suggest, that the homing travellers have been in committee in saloon and deck chair. The agenda of these committees is invariably the same. How much, the question rises, of what is, according to the strict letter of the law, dutiable will the Customs allow through by gentlemen's agreement. A supplementary question, put more shyly, is, in blunt colloquial English, how much extra can one get away with, undetected. Admissions come to light in the course of discussion of this or that article cunningly hidden in the recesses of the speaker's largest suitcase that will not be declared.

Guilt complex is smothered by the comforting reflection that those Customs chaps have a sixth sense for telling real crooks and that they tolerate, open eyed, the small amateur of evasion. What they are really after, the talk on board proceeds, is big stuff—drugs, jewels, three-figure bank notes. The temporary woman criminal comforts herself with the reflection that she would not know hashish from heroin if they were offered to her on a

111

plate and that she has never seen £100 on a single sheet of paper in her life. This consciousness of purity and austerity fortifies her as she looks lovingly at the new wrist watch she is wearing and remembers the nylons wrapped in the linen that is to go to the laundry. Her husband, taking a pull at the brandy bottle, so that if it is unearthed from between his shirts it will at least be shown to have been broached, buttresses his self-respect by recalling that he resisted temptation over a box of cigars. An ugly moment comes to all conspirators when they are handed across the counter that solemn declaration set out in large type, that adjures them to " come clean " or to take the consequences without being able to pretend that they did not know what they were doing. Faint hearts beat quickly until the chalk cross blesses transgression and the plunder is safely lodged on the rack of the train. It is all very wrong, but the article that is not declared is rarely of much value ; the wish to smuggle in this small way springs from sporting rather than mercenary instincts.

AUTOBIOGRAPHY FOR OFFICERS

Considering how fond we all are of talking about ourselves, and even in some cases of writing about ourselves, it might have been supposed that Army Form B 199A (Revised 1949) would have been assured of a warm welcome. For this spacious document is intended to elicit from the officer all the particulars of his career in the service, so that his personal records at the War Office may be amplified, corrected, and brought up to date. Ardently though holders of HIS MAJESTY'S commission revere the department over which MR. STRACHEY now presides, there is sometimes a disposition on the part of individuals to feel that the paternal interest taken by the War Office in their careers is not always based on a just appreciation of their own attainments; and when the keen young officer who has just qualified as an interpreter in Cantonese is posted to Nigeria he is tempted to wonder whether his own limited understanding will ever be able to fathom the inscrutable wisdom of Whitehall.

So an opportunity of putting the Army Council in the picture is one which most officers will welcome in principle. In practice, however, the Army form provided for the purpose may rather cool their autobiographical zeal. They will be flattered to note that the record of their past promotions includes a space for the effective date of their elevation to the rank of field-marshal; and they may not take altogether amiss the veiled charge of forgery implicit in

Date of Birth (a) Actual......
(b) Declared......

for it sounds as if the General Staff suspects them of nothing worse than the patriotic peccadillo of joining the colours while legally under age to do so. But some of them

H

—especially those whose service has been long and honourable—may feel slightly aggrieved, after reading the instruction " Every effort will be made to enter the following occurrences in chronological order," to see that the fifteen episodes which the War Office apparently regards as more or less normal in an officer's career include both cashiering and dismissal.

They will be mystified, too, by the injunction to write their permanent address in pencil rather than ink ; some of them may not be able—offhand—to comply with the order " The optical standard of each eye without glasses will be written above the dotted lines and standard with glasses beneath these dotted lines " ; and when they read " Nationality will be shown as ' English,' ' Irish,' ' Maltese,' &c., and not as ' British,' " they may be temporarily distracted by a mental vision of a bespectacled Maltese field-marshal being cashiered on his (declared) birthday. The reference to " the current profession or trade (if any) of an officer of the Reserve or Territorial Forces " may strike them as containing an implied slur on these piping times of full employment ; and, though they will welcome the chance of telling the War Office about " any extraordinary journeys or remote places visited before joining the Army," and though few of them will find much difficulty in " making a distinction between such journeys as a P. & O. tour around the world and a journey to the Polar regions with an exploring expedition " (for these two types of experience are seldom inextricably confused in a man's mind), it will not be until they reach the last entry—" 32. Record of Occurrences not Shown at Serials 1-31 "—that most officers will be able to expatiate on achievements of which they feel not enough cognizance has been taken. Here is the place for unsung triumphs and neglected feats ; and if any officer puts down " Completion of AF B 199A (Revised 1949) " he can hardly be held to be claiming credit for a trivial achievement.

REBELLIOUS YOUTH

There are some things as to which it is on the whole pleasant to reflect that they never can happen again. One of them is the entering an examination room to find a paper set with palpably malignant intent and containing, as sorrow's crown of sorrow, one question which the candidate had intended to look up and had then too light-heartedly forgotten. But even in these infuriating circumstances few of us ever seriously contemplated shooting the invigilating demon and destroying the papers or the examination chamber. We had not half the enterprise attributed to some Egyptian students of commercial subjects in Cairo. Finding the papers not at all the esteemed favours they had expected they burnt them and then, it is reported, inspired by the cheerful crackling, tried to set a light to the building as well. That was, no doubt, going too far. It was a piece of audacity comparable to that of the boy who let off fireworks on DR. KEATE'S lawn on Guy Fawkes day. Nevertheless there is here something fine and independent, reminiscent of the old spirit of barring-out to be found in ancient school stories, including one of MISS EDGEWORTH'S, which used to make the nursery blood dance in the veins.

Nor were these dashing antics by any means confined to literature. Witness for instance the great rebellion against DR. FOSTER at Eton in 1768. It was no merely pedantic complaint against examination papers that stirred it, but rather one as to the liberty of the subject. A hundred and sixty boys first performed the symbolic act of throwing their school books over Windsor Bridge and then marched " with the greatest order and regularity " to Maidenhead. There they ran up a bill of some £55 for two nights at the inn and then marched away again

115

to meet with fates various, but on the whole humiliating. " You shall go to the play to-night for your pleasure," said one parent, " and to-morrow you shall return to Dr. Foster and be flogged for mine." That was as a rule the end of these adventures, which generally failed from some unheroic oversight, such as that at Armagh, described in the late MR. STEUART TRENCH'S reminiscences, where the rebels had laid in vast stocks of food and sparrow-hail with which to shoot at the authorities' legs, but no water to drink. The young commercial gentlemen of Cairo are presumably too old to be flogged, but the examiners can twist their tails for them by papers infinitely worse than the first, a venomous account rendered.

THE DONKEY AND THE BEETLES

When we talk about incentives—a habit which seems to be growing on us—there is one which we never mention. We speak of the profit-motive, of the competitive spirit, of *esprit de corps*, of nest-eggs and rainy days, of the carrot and (reluctantly) the stick. But we never talk about bribes. We have heard, of course, that such things exist in other countries, where they are brazenly offered and shamelessly accepted at all levels in the community. Baksheesh and squeeze are, we have long understood, the principal agencies by which the gorgeous East is held in fee ; and although in our own Empire we hold dominion over palm and pine without being obliged more or less continuously to grease the former, we are regretfully aware that other parts of the world are less immune from corrupt practices. This knowledge induces a feeling of self-righteousness.

To the foreign connoisseur of British hypocrisy it will thus come as no surprise to learn that there is no Briton (over the age of about two and a half) who has not been bribed, and that bribery of the lower age-groups by their seniors is an accepted feature of our family life, supposedly so unblemished and *comme il faut*. It begins, in a small way, with sweets, but the currency of these equivocal transactions grows both in variety and value as the cupidity of the beneficiaries develops. The young citizen who, a year or two back, was content to settle for a bull's-eye soon learns to raise the ante, quickly apprehending that the grown-up who offers him a penny to go away and play at the other end of the garden might just as well make it sixpence. And so it goes on in a vicious spiral—on and on and on and up and up and up. The young blackmailer (for that is really what—thanks

117

to us—he is) adjusts his incentive-rate with extortionate opportunism. What he got for counting up to ten will by no means recompense more strenuous intellectual feats ; and the paltry Danegeld for which he was prepared to remove himself from our presence is not enough to reward his services in the matter of posting a letter.

It is accordingly with envious amazement that many will have read of the incentive-rates prevailing among Belgian children, who have been mobilized to combat the menace of the Colorado beetle at Ostend. Each child is to receive one free donkey-ride for every hundred of these noxious insects which it collects. Without seeming in any way to under-value the pleasures of riding upon a donkey, it must be observed that this contract exhibits the negotiating powers of the grown-ups in an unprecedentedly favourable light. A beetle-throughput running into three figures is after all no mean target ; and donkeys, though endearing, can hardly be regarded, as methods of locomotion go, as approximating to the *dernier cri*. One of the more terrifying types of scenic railway, or a speed-boat, or a helicopter—these are more the kinds of conveyance which would have been needed to stimulate the civic conscience of the British child ; and, though it is pleasant as well as unusual to find a donkey playing the part of a carrot, one somehow feels that it may not prove indefinitely equal to the role.

STRANGER IN THESE PARTS

Week-ends in June give the explorer at the wheel or on foot his most leisurely chance of getting off the beaten British track by daylight—and of getting lost. Travel through forest and jungle is, by comparison, child's play. All the far-flung pioneer has to do, when in doubt, is to follow his compass bearing and, sooner or later, even if months later, he is able to come home and ask us to judge of his surprise and joy on sighting the majestic curves of the Congo or the mud huts clustering round the mission station. A compass is no good when a short cut is being taken to reach Brighton in time for tea. A 1in. ordnance map, fondly though many walkers delude themselves into believing that they can read it, is no better. That, they say, tracing a blurred line with their finger, is obviously a bridle-path, leading over the Downs to the main road a mile this side of that railway cutting. Whether or no it is what they think and not, as is more probable, a county boundary makes no odds. The party finds itself adrift with an impenetrable spinney ahead and a watchful bull in the neighbouring field.

Motorists fare no better, for they, too, are the victims of pipe dreams. They maintain, in the teeth of back seat opposition that, in open country, they can steer by sign posts and, through towns, they can follow those complicated little street plans gummed into all the best guide books. Now that milestones have been more or less superseded, the road to Roundabout is freely ornamented by signs at various heights and often with conflicting information. Their erection has, no doubt, given the various central and local authorities responsible much food for thought, and although they do not always tell the same story and sometimes, apparently tiring of a name, drop it just when it is most needed, they would serve any motorist who had the patience to stop and consider. Unfortunately the man who is prepared really to pause at an enigmatic parting of the ways has yet to pass his driving test. Impatience hurries him off course, just as, in a few minutes, it is going to bring him into conflict with the policeman on point duty at the corner of the one way traffic street he is briskly negotiating against its appointed flow through the medieval gyrations of the cathedral city. As he reverses and is warned not to do so by a hoot from the old clergyman behind in a vehicle that must have been on its wheels when red flags were *de rigueur*, he is taught a lesson that he should, and will not, remember.

The iron curtain of reticence, lowered over British roads in war-time, had its advantages. There was a thoroughness about it, bred of a deep insular love for fooling the stranger. No chances were taken of helping the enemy anywhere from John o' Groats to Land's End. Had he descended from his parachute in the tiniest village the front of the post office would have stared at him in blank silence. Had he landed rather nearer the bull's eye and sunk into one of the benches in the gardens by the Tower, he would have found the name on it conscientiously deleted. Many Londoners chuckled, even in that summer ten years ago, at the vision of an invader thus baffled for lack of written direction under the walls of the historic fortress. Now that too much rather than too little guidance is displayed, the wise explorer stops and asks and, every now and then, does not pick on another stranger in those parts.

SHAVING MADE DIFFICULT

MR. ARNOLD BENNETT improved his French by conning as he shaved a list of words set up at the side of his shaving mirror. That his good example is not more widely followed is due, we may be sure, rather to a shortage of time than to any lack of enthusiasm for the pursuit of learning. The odd moments which MR. BENNETT desired so ardently to make the most of become, alas, scarcer and scarcer. The ordinary shaver (using the word in its adult sense) has little time for French ; his aim is only to complete the morning toilet with as much speed and as little bloodshed as possible and rapidly to remove himself to the place where he earns what is still described as his " living."

The manufacturers of shaving accessories do their utmost to aid him in this object. They do not expect him to linger lovingly among their products, but seek unselfishly and constantly to discover gadgets and processes that will enable him to knock a few more seconds off his record time. That less speed issues from his greater haste, that breakdowns almost daily interrupt his passage from the disreputable to the respectable, is not their fault. The directions they provide are clear and simple, and now and then he reads them, but Nature has left him strangely ill-equipped for carrying them out.

He has formed the habit, for instance, of buying his shaving soap in tubes. He knows well enough what he ought to do. What could be simpler than first to press gently at the tail of the tube, and gradually to work towards the mouth, and neatly to roll the whole thing up as it empties day by day ? There must be many good citizens who really do this, but he is not of their conscientious company. The temptation to begin by squeezing

121

in the middle is always irresistible; and thereafter he proceeds at random, pressing lightly here and digging more viciously there, till the tube takes on a shape unknown to geometry and soap is shooting forth from half a dozen unscheduled points. Obvious remedies will at once suggest themselves to logical minds; some of them occur from time to time to the bungler himself; but the problem is one of habit and temperament and not of logic; and reform, one fears, will be long delayed.

WEIGHTS AND PLEASURES

Alcohol to the value of between 700 and 800 calories, says authority, was consumed, before the war, at an average dinner. Reminiscent topers may be puzzled to impale that " average " between the horns of a narrow bracket. A few diners drank nothing, some drank water, and others drank as often and as quickly as they could catch the eye of the wine waiter. Six-bottle men went out before living memory, but their drier descendants of yesterday, free from the expensive duty of fortifying the Exchequer to over-proof strength with every glassful, still did pretty well for themselves. The moral of authority is easier to follow than are its reported figures and it may bring comfort to some quisling Falstaffs, torn in their loyalty between affection for the bottle and fear of growing fatter. However much exercise is taken—so the latest if not the novel fiat has gone forth—the athlete must not hope to regain, or at least to retain the slim, willowy lines traceable in the fading photographs of his youth.

Let a man row from Putney to Mortlake nine times and he will get up such an appetite in the process that his last and postprandial state will be worse than that in which he waddled to the boat. Let him play squash rackets for half an hour and a pint of beer or a double whisky and soda or two slices of bread and butter will, so far as the scales take an interest in him, undo all the good work. The argument is clinched by pointing to those happy idlers who have, it seems, only to stay in their beds in order rapidly to bring down their weights. Why in the face of such evidence should the stones not be left to turn themselves off when nature wants them to and not before ?

123

Why should avenues of distasteful exercise be strenuously explored, if they are all sure to end in the same *cul de sac* ? Laymen, too puny to be strokes and too plump to be coxes, have often appeased a sense of inferiority by noticing, or affecting to notice, that the brawny muscles, which any coach worth his salt grafts on to his victims, turn, before the summer is out, into undeniably adipose tissue. Now science has come to the support of this agreeable theory.

Fat men will be amused, but not dismayed. They are merry gentlemen. Optimism, determination and a fiery individualism are their birthright. The secret stores of creative energy, denied to leaner bodies, that have made them what they are, act on the spirit no less than on the flesh. May be, they will say, this craven invitation to sloth has something in it, but authority has not always spoken, and will not invariably speak, with the same voice. Even if it did, who among the choicest bearers of great weight will be downcast ? The cold bath and the skipping rope in town, the brisk trot before breakfast in the country are not ordeals lightly to be abandoned. Total abstention from this and that food or drink and a cunning, if spartan dietary combination of others may —who knows ?—do the trick. The thin man might be " hudden doon " by experience ; nothing could prevail against his more robust opposite number who dismisses as featherweight the (perhaps) transitory evidence of the unforgiving scales.

124

GOOD LOSERS

The British are a self-distrustful, diffident people, agreeing with alacrity that they are neither successful nor clever and only modestly claiming that they have a keener sense of humour, more robust common sense, and greater staying power as a nation than all the rest of the world put together. Long practice in defeat at every kind of sport has led them to accept the downfall of their champions with the utmost *bonhomie*, but it has also left them embarrassed and ill at ease when, as happens every now and then, they win. If a French horse gallops home first in the Derby a thousand and one good reasons are promptly brought forward to explain how natural this is and how likely it is to happen again and again. An American boxer takes without any visible signs of discomfort everything that his British opponent can give him on the chin and then retaliates with swiftly decisive punishment. Insular football teams venturing on to the Continent are trounced by Ruritania. Experts are never at a loss to explain on such occasions that the selection committees, the methods of training, and the general deplorably low level of the game with which the losers are content among themselves make it surprising that they did not do even worse against their oversea hosts or visitors. Nemesis every now and then catches up these gaily confident analysts of decline and fall. They have to explain away a victory.

They were looking back complacently on Epsom, the Davis Cup, and the Open Golf Championship, and sharpening their pencils or oiling their typewriters to record the (no doubt) coming *débcâle* at Wimbledon, when an exception happened to disturb the rules.

England won a Test match. Happily an excuse, a convincing excuse, was to hand. The wicket had been so scientifically tended that its last state was much like that of the unfortunates in *The Cocktail Party* after they had fallen into the clutches of the psychiatrist. This alibi to explain how England came to play truant from defeat is weighty and the West Indies deserve, as they have amply received, the commiserations of all cricketers. Still, it has certainly got the commentators out of a hole.

A match in which only two short of a thousand runs were scored would not have seemed to old-fashioned county players to reveal a bias on the part of the wicket in favour of the fielding side. There are, even in these days of pampered pitches, club and village grounds with the boundary much nearer to the batsman than it is at Old Trafford and on which a thousand runs are seldom scored in a month of Saturdays. What the clubs and villages say is not evidence ; only the best is good enough for first-class cricketers and that they evidently did not get in Lancashire. The critics can breathe again, but they must be left with an uneasy feeling. Suppose some gigantic island infant, now crushing its rattle in a chubby but already oversized fist, grows up into a heavyweight to knock out all comers ? Who knows whether a greater than Eclipse has not lately been foaled ? Disaster may be nearer still ; next winter may bring back the Ashes from Australia.

THE SPORTING RUMANIANS

The Committee for Physical Culture and Sport of the Council of Ministers of the Rumanian People's Republic has lately set up a State Sports Association. This will be known as the " Ready to Work and Defend the Rumanian People's Republic " Association, which will minimize the danger of anybody mixing it up with the M.C.C. or the Jockey Club. It differs, as a matter of fact, from these bodies in various other ways as well. Membership is compulsory for those who wish to take part in any form of sport, and the primary purpose of the association is defined as being " to educate workers in a spirit of true patriotism and proletarian ethics, in a spirit of unbounded love for the Soviet Union and its great leader, Joseph Vissarionovitch Stalin." Other objects are " the development of the technique of exercises of a utility character " and " the maintenance of hygiene." All members are enjoined " to combat cosmopolitanism in sport, expressed by servility to the decadent sport of the West."

In spite of this last, rather wounding thrust, the formation of the Rumanian State Sports Association will be unreservedly welcomed in this country. It is not merely that any cause devoted to the maintenance of hygiene in that romantic country automatically commands our support ; it is not merely that we hope that our own feelings for MR. STALIN, which are too often inexcusably tepid, will be compensated for by the unstinted adoration of countless Rumanian athletes ; it is not that we know, or even care, what sports are practised in Rumania, or look forward to the day when they will ask us to come and play them at whatever it is they do play. The pleasure we derive from this latest move in Rumania is the sort

127

of rather base pleasure that is felt by a gentleman who, while escorting at Ascot a young lady in a particularly silly hat, suddenly sees another gentleman whose companion is wearing an even sillier one. We know—or at least we ought to know, for we are told it very often—that we take sport too seriously, that we are constantly making ourselves ridiculous by our enthusiasms and our pedantries, our controversies and taboos and reminiscences. So that when something like the Rumanian State Sports Association comes along, and we get a glimpse of the great gulf of claptrap and mumbo-jumbo which underlies it, we have—fleetingly—an access of confidence in our own sense of proportion and it is with a feeling almost of self-righteousness that we take the afternoon off to go and watch a game of cricket.

DANGEROUS FRIENDS

" To prevent your people at home," said Dr. Grimston, " from being shocked and distressed in future by the crudity of your communications, I have drawn up a short form of letter which I shall now proceed to dictate." There are times when we should all be grateful for the doctor's help in composing certain kinds of letter due on traditional occasions. There is the letter of condolence too painful to dwell upon. There is that of congratulation, which ought not to demand any great skill, since the recipient will be in no hypercritical mood ; yet it is possible to offend by showing too obvious a surprise at his success. There is the bread and butter letter or Collins, of which as a rule the first sentence flows much more trippingly from the pen than does the second. According to SIR WALTER RALEIGH " A Collins should not wade into deep places. It should be loving but neat." No doubt he had a high standard, but the ordinary mortal should come to no great harm, so long as he remembers not to give a minute account of his catching the 12.52 at the junction on his way home. There is yet another form of letter which is superficially simple enough and yet will often be found to prove all the hard things that have been said about good intentions. This is the letter which a proposer or seconder writes in support of his candidate for a club or other such association.

It may well be that the auditors who have to listen to it grow weary and so too critical, and yet it would seem, mysteriously enough, that this is an occasion on which the writer is suddenly bereft of his wits. Indeed he might almost be suspected of that acme of treachery, the desire to secure his own man's rejection. Sometimes he will write briefly that he considers the candidate highly eligible, giving no particulars, but suggesting that his praise is praise indeed and therefore suffices ; and sure enough it does suffice to infuriate the hearers. Sometimes again he goes to the opposite extreme—to be sure a fault on the right side—beginning with his man's private school and tracing him through three changes of profession to his ultimate eminence. In some incredible manner he can state the poor wretch's solid qualities so as to make him appear that dread phenomenon, " a prince of good fellows." He can laud his cultivated interests so that he must inevitably be a prig and a bore. Yet worse than any of these styles is the deliberately facetious which shows what a clever fellow is the writer and would ensure the defeat of an angel supported by several archangels. In all these cases if only the victim knew he would exclaim passionately

Save me, oh, save me from the candid friend.

RURAL INTERLUDE

When branches in May are torn from the tree trunks
by a weight of snow pressing on their leaves and, a week
or so later, thrushes sit with beaks agape, nursing their
eggs in the heat of the day, a temperate English summer
has got into its stride. Now, with the hay mostly in and
the short-tailed fledglings out and about, offering themselves as hostages to fortune in every lane, there is a pause
before the mechanized armies of reapers invade the corn-
fields. Farmers, whose work, like that of housewives, is
never done, cannot sit back, but the idle observer may see
in these long midsummer days, better perhaps than at any
other stage of the year, the pattern of the new countryside.

Free-flowing petrol has already made a change. Lorries,
trailers, and cattle vans are increasingly joined by the
veteran family car with gaily carolling wireless and
perilously wobbling wheels. These resurrected birds of
passage will, unless, as is only too probable, they collide
with one another in their quest for solitude, be gone by
supper time. By then the windows of the great house
are dark, unless it has been converted into an institution
or a preparatory school. There is a light in the vicarage—
built for six servants at a gross wages bill of about £150
a year—and it shines from the kitchen, where the vicar's
wife is doing the ironing. The village hall is in the occu-
pation of parish councillors, some of whom, by a
conspicuous break with tradition, seem younger than the
average justice of the peace. They are debating fiercely
about footpaths. They have, which they seldom used to
have, a small audience. Members of the Women's
Institute, who in the afternoon were discussing, in the
same arena and with equal zest, juvenile delinquents or
rug-making, are (unless they are councillors) back at

131

home and (like their tireless colleague, the vicar's wife) doing the ironing. Members of the Young Farmers' Club have gone into the market town on their motor-bicycles to hear a talk on how to judge the points of a pig. Cottage gardens are being brooded over by their owners, before whose eyes dance the first-prize cards of next month's flower show. Vegetables, prodigious in size and marvellously symmetrical, lie hidden in those beds. Kindly fruits of the earth that will yield, when pressed to do so, treacherous alcoholic vintages, demurely disguised under reassuring rustic names, are still unripe.

The new countryside has, like the corn and the fruit, a long way to go before it reaches the maturity of harvest, but never has the old seemed more remote, and most villagers are happy in the change. They have pretty well laid the ghost of the inferiority complex that used to send their sons and daughters flocking into the towns. When they grumble, as they do every day, it is for some of the same reasons that upset townsmen. What they say before closing time about Ministerial forms would be ruled out by MR. SPEAKER as unparliamentary. Their views on housing are no less forthright, but they believe, as they did not always in the past, that they are a power in, as well as on, the land. They mean to get indoor sanitation and running water, and they expect, sooner or later, to have television aerials rather than thatch on their roofs. They are sons of their fathers and proud to grow, round the doors of a council house, roses as English and as unofficial as those that bloomed in the Grantchester of RUPERT BROOKE.

TIDINGS

This is a time of year at which a considerable proportion of the population finds itself involved in the organization of pageants. Nobody knows at what stage in its history our extraordinary race acquired this habit of reproducing, generally in a light but wetting rain, painstaking travesties of past events ; but the practice has clearly come to stay, and if it is not so rife as usual in 1950 there is every reason to fear that it will be rifer than ever in 1951. In order to stage a pageant it is first necessary to select a site on which to stage it, a task full of difficulties, upon which, however, the project all too seldom founders. The park of a gentleman's residence is still much sought after as a *venue* and, provided it is not being used for opencast mining, an assault course, or the housing of foreign workers in Nissen huts, such a setting has a great deal to be said for it.

The organizer of experience and discrimination will automatically have secured the support of an influential committee before embarking on his grand design. In addition to this volatile and often acrimonious body he will require the services of an old grey horse, such an animal being for some reason indispensable to any revival of the glories of the past. He will need—theoretically—an author and a historical adviser, but most organizers prefer to keep these vital portfolios in their own hands. In the selection of dramatic episodes from local history the main prerequisite is an open mind and a nimble imagination, for it is surprising in how many localities, all down the chequered, violent, splendid centuries of our

133

rough island story, nothing of the slightest interest seems to have happened. Never sacked by the Danes, by-passed by the Black Death, just over the border of PRINCE RUPERT's Friday country, religiously shunned by itinerant royalty, without even a minor poet in the graveyard, many an English village has slumbered on without acquiring the most abstruse, the most indirect claim to fame or notoriety.

This does not deter pageant-fanciers in the least. It acts, rather, as a challenge. The fact that nothing ever happened at Scribblebury does not mean that its inhabitants stood altogether aloof from the great cavalcade of English history. Far from it. They were frequently —indeed, it would appear almost incessantly—receiving news (technically known as tidings) of tremendous events. The Danes have landed ! The Normans have landed ! The Armada has been sighted ! The Round-heads are coming ! Barefooted over the ancient green-sward pants the postman's son, praying that the safety-pins will hold his garment of sheepskin in its place. See how frantically he points to the eastward, see (as far as their huge false beards will allow it) the consternation on the faces of the Ancient Scribbleburians as the full import of his tidings bursts upon them ! Above the pattering of the rain upon our umbrellas we can hear them crying " The Danes ! The Danes ! " as, picking up their spears and their little stools and their cooking pot, they go shambling off into the middle distance at that rather furtive, gliding trot which is so integral a feature of all histrionics in the open air. . . . And now several more centuries have rolled by and, just as we have congratu-lated ourselves on identifying the curious object on the wrist of the gentleman in a doublet as the stuffed kestrel from the bar-parlour of the Dog and Duck, the idyllic glimpse of Scribblebury under Good Queen Bess is once

134

more galvanized into drama ; for there, thundering stertorously up the lime avenue, is the old grey horse bearing a young lady from the pony club dressed as a cross between Dick Whittington and a beefeater, and again there is a great deal of pointing and gesticulating, and everybody who can draws his sword, and as they all stumble away we can hear that they are intoning " The Armada ! The Armada ! " in a rather aggressive way. Once more history has come to Scribblebury—or should it be the other way round ?

PAPER CHASE

It must have been with something of the slightly vulgar curiosity evoked by the details of other people's wills that the British public studied the particulars revealed the other day by SIR STAFFORD CRIPPS of the varying tonnages of paper used during 1949 by the departments of HIS MAJESTY's Government. Between them they got through just under 40,000 tons. To some people this figure will seem disgracefully high, to others remarkably low, this wide divergence of views being due to the fact that very few of us are capable of, so to speak, rendering down a ton of paper into sub-units which are within our own comprehension. None of us, for instance, knows how much paper he or she used in 1949. All the letters that we wrote, all the parcels we wrapped up at Christmas, the exercise books we got for the children, the hats out of the crackers, the pages of our pocket diary, the race-cards, the theatre programmes, the tickets given us by cloakroom attendants—as we look back on the paper we consumed we find it extraordinarily difficult to assess it in terms of avoirdupois. A hundredweight? It sounds a lot in one way, not very much in another. We really prefer not to make an estimate.

This culpable vagueness is not, fortunately, shared by our rulers, and SIR STAFFORD CRIPPS's list is full of suggestive data. Far and away the biggest bull in the paper market is the POSTMASTER-GENERAL, who, besides using up 3,720 tons on (one presumes) postage stamps and telegraph forms, converted a further 8,460 tons into telephone directories, at least some of the numbers in which we remember to have been quite frequently, if not very quickly, available during 1949. It is a little surprising to find the MINISTER of HEALTH at the bottom of the poll with only 260 tons, and farmers, who are better judges of a ton than most people, will be astonished to learn that the Ministry of Agriculture and Fisheries used only 800 tons. It felt like much more. Anybody who has had any dealings with the Ministry of Town and Country Planning will be unfavourably impressed by its failure—apparently —to divulge the details of its paper consumption ; neither it nor the Home Office figures on SIR STAFFORD CRIPPS'S list and his total must accordingly be accepted with reserve.

Pride rather than amazement will be the dominant emotion in soldiers who note that the War Office, notching 4,560 tons, was nearly 2,000 tons ahead of either of the other service departments ; the General Staff, never niggardly in its distribution of paper during the stern years of war, is clearly determined that there shall be no relaxation of its standards in the softer atmosphere of peace. The Foreign Office might perhaps have got by on less than 1,680 tons if it had departed from its practice of using rather long words, but this would probably have been a false economy in the long run. On the whole, most Britons will feel that a Government which can rule 50m. people for 365 days with 40,000 tons of paper is not doing too badly. It works out at roughly two pounds of paper for each citizen, which is equivalent to ten average copies of *The Times*—speaking strictly in quantitative terms, of course.

AMONG OUR SOUVENIRS

Ever since our nursery days there has been conflict with that impossible axiom : " A place for everything and everything in its place." Not that we find it less than admirable, merely a little more than humanly possible. The muddle about us shows no sign of lessening, or indeed of anything but a temporary abatement, however hard we try to be tidy. What in the end defeats us is not the abundance of our possessions, or their lack of rightful places, but simply that we seem unable to avoid becoming the natural heirs of accumulated residue, the quite unnecessary but no less inevitable salvage of past encounters and pursuits. Our attics become impassable, our drawers and cupboards overflowing, with this hoarded sediment of time. It seems no home can ever be designed to hold without distress the unlikely lumber that a man gathers in his journeying.

Nor is it much better when, generally under orders but sometimes by the stirring of conscience, a clearance is attempted. We have not for this work the quality of non-attachment displayed by the gentleman in MAURICE BARING'S story who spent several intoxicated weeks burning the manuscripts of the library of Alexandria, ending up, so he said, with the private diary of JULIUS CAESAR. Our own accretions of diaries and manuscripts are of less importance—indeed if we are honest we can admit that they are of no importance whatsoever—yet they are not for sale nor for the incinerator. Wistfully they stare at us from their newly discovered hiding places, these curious, pathetic relics of time past, and having come across them after such a long separation we are reluctant to commit them to oblivion. We may have started out well enough on our clearing up, but each discovery will give us pause. Who can really be certain that this or that will not, some day, come in useful? We cannot say. On the other hand, one never knows. No man, we find, can be ruthless with his souvenirs. If the house is not big enough for them, if there are not enough places to go round, then we must relax our standards of tidiness a little, if only to provide one more pleasant rummage on some rainy afternoon.

MARKED FOR LIFE

The writer of a letter published recently in *The Times*, complained that the marking of linen by laundries left much to be desired. It was suggested that the mystic symbols, many of which would feel at home in a quadratic equation, were bold, obtrusive and virtually ineradicable ; it was inferred that they had palpably not been subjected to any planning laws in the matter of siting. In reply the secretary of the Institution of British Launderers defended the mystical alphabet used in the trade and maintained that laundry marks were in general as small as was consistent with clarity. The criticism and the defence suggest that a compromise might be found were both parties to introduce a little more imagination and give rein to their aesthetic instincts. Could not a customer design his own insignia—J. Doe, his mark—which could be cunningly worked in petit-point on the border of his only remaining lace-edged table-cloth ? Could it not be knitted tastefully into the webbing of his pyjama cord, emblazoned on the bosom of his spare room bedspread, or crocheted in a chaste pattern on the obverse of his vests?

The historian's pleasure can be derived from a close study of laundry markings. Shirts, collars (semi-stiff), and towels can, like the pyramids, summon up remembrance of things past through a peculiarly personal language. The laundry's shorthand can unfold a personal tapestry in the mind. The purple symbol on the edge of the handkerchief speaks of 1939 and the work of that laundry that served up shirts girt with coloured bands of paper like regal orders, and parcelled them up in shiny paper, closely pinned, like a florist's orchids. The copperplate squiggle in ink is the signature of a small town laundry visited hurriedly before being shipped to foreign parts during the war. The muddy patch farther along the hem is no laundry mark but the blood of a tropical insect that foolishly lolled overlong on the handkerchief after the owner had purged it in aircraft petrol, laved it in water, and laid it in the sun to dry. Last comes some neat figuring with a seven crossed like the letter " F " ; another land but a more sophisticated laundry, staffed by fifteen frauleins kept like chickens in an old ammunition shed in a captured German camp. That is the end of the line, for the coffee-brown star with points that would do credit to a stag brings the wheel full cycle. It is the mark of the owner, recording a return to days of peace and extreme penury, a period of every-man-his-own-launderer, cleansing personal linen the hard way with nail brush, intractable kitchen soap, and some pumice stone. It appears that a new system, now in its experimental stages, may eventually obviate the naming, tabbing, the numbering and marking, but there will be some who will regret when it will no longer be possible to assess the antiquity of a garment, like a silver teapot, by the marks.

SPEECH DAY

The little imp of ubiquity without whose help no novel could be written must enjoy himself on these midsummer Saturday mornings. He is fortunately endowed with the powers of being in several places at once, of over-hearing domestic conversations, and even of attending a close up, private view of the hopes and views running through the minds of his victims. If he is now on a five-day week and can snap his fingers on Saturdays at novelists stumped for copy, he may well take a busman's holiday on his own and do a round of the schools. One or other of them is certain by breakfast time to be sickening for its Speech Day and the imp— if no one else, from the Chairman of the Board of Governors to the groundsman's boy—is in for a good time.

He will begin with the distinguished Old Boy who, as he shaves, is mentally putting the last touches to the few well-chosen words with which he must, in an hour or so, address the mob of veterans and teen-agers in Founder's Hall. The twin, bewhiskered assertions that schooldays are the happiest time of life and that the great man never himself won a prize have been abandoned, partly because they are both untrue and partly on the score of age. The thesis that we live in a world of changing values but that " Floreat " is still the word for their own and lesser schools is true enough and, yet, could be made to sound familiar. Leaving the speaker-to-be to these perplexities, the imp now looks in on the select band of orators whose misery mounts as the zero hour approaches for their recitations in Greek, Latin, French, and even English. They remember, nostalgically, care-free vanished Junes in which they were able to sit back when the hush fell and their predecessors on the sacrificial altar of tradition wrestled like Homeric heroes with purple passages from the Iliad and just did not dry up in the middle of Henry V's remarks before Harfleur. Juniors who have not got this year to show the mettle of their pasture on the platform might be expected by mothers and fathers to be the next port of call for the roving imp. Instead, he makes for mothers and fathers, pursuing them in his unfeeling way into the recesses of their bedrooms.

It is a parental illusion that small boys lose appetite at breakfast on Speech Day for fear a too juvenile frock or an unhappily chosen hat will lower the family flag. The bedroom looking-glass is called in as consultant, husbands give unhelpful answers to appeals for advice, and wives, surveying their partners, tell them that they cannot possibly sally forth for the ordeal in that disgraceful suit. Nerves remain taut until a quickly appraising and, if luck is in, approving glance, as generations meet, shows that dressmaker and tailor have come up to Fourth Form standards. After that the imp must mingle with the crowd, watching parents eye one another with speculative hostility, boys raise caps to the parents of other boys, equally a prey to this abnormal politeness, and harassed masters in full academic fig, determined to steer clear of any entangling *tête-à-tête* about their pupils. The imp retires cheerfully to bed. He will be back on Monday to his work for the novelists—a giant refreshed.

CHRISTIAN NAMES

SIR PELHAM WARNER deprecated the use of Christian names in cricket broadcast commentaries the other day. The use of Christian names has increased, is increasing and ought to be diminished. There have always been those who have spoken of the great they have never met in terms which suggest the closest of friendships, and the deception is harmless enough, although the nickname is more appropriate for this mild form of vanity. HAZLITT may, in general, have been right in declaring that a nickname is the heaviest stone the devil can throw at a man, but there is nevertheless something endearing about nicknames, and the pity is that invention of them seems to be a dying art. The " Coroner," the " Croucher," the " Guv'nor," " Plum " himself, and, to go back in time to a different age and art, the " Game Chicken " and the " Gasman," set their mark on the imagination of their contemporaries. How much more vivid and impressive they are than any amount of Lens and Dennises, of Bruces and Lees.

It is a sign of progress and enlightenment in education and upbringing that the very existence to a small boy of a Christian name should no longer be looked upon as something shameful, a dread secret only to be divulged under frightful oaths of secrecy to the blood-brother of the hour, and the step from the cosy Christian-name atmosphere of nursery and school-room to the bleak surname world of the preparatory school was precipitous. It is as well that the rigid taboo should be relaxed, although doubtless it is in places still strict enough, but in adult life the revolution has gone altogether too far. If the crowd is not satisfied with the surnames of its sporting heroes unadorned, there are always initials—and initials were

144

once charged with charm and potency. What mere name can rival the impressiveness of C. B. FRY, L. C. H. PALAIRET, J. T. TYLDESLEY or J. T. HEARNE ? But to-day it must be Tom, Dick and Harry, and soon the only really distinguished person left will be the convict rejoicing in the austere and dignified anonymity of a number.

K

DEARER HANDKERCHIEFS

The Board of Trade has spoken and up goes the price of handkerchiefs, or at any rate that of some utility cotton ones. This is one of the blows which in these hard times may be confidently expected and must be philosophically endured. It would be futile to adopt an heroic attitude and declare that we will do without a handkerchief. It is one of the few essentials of life that cannot be dispensed with. True we may for a moment escape. It sometimes happened to us to go into school with our lesson wholly unprepared and not to be put on to construe. Similarly we may forget our handkerchief and be troubled with never a single snuffle all day long, but this is unlikely ; the Fates mark down those who thus openly flout them. So it was with Kipps when he cut his wrist in trying to open a window for the divine Miss Walshingham, and had to stanch the blood by a neat process of licking. " Not 'aving a cold, I suppose some'ow I didn't think ——" he had to explain ; it was all extremely embarrassing.

Those old enough to have seen the beloved CORNEY GRAIN may remember his impersonation of a small, cross child, who after flouncing about the room and emitting a series of terrific sniffs exclaimed in a venomous tone " Well, I haven't got one then ! " It is a thing that may happen to any one of us, to find himself in the case of the little vulgar boy on Margate pier who

Had no little handkerchief to wipe his little nose.

Yet the predicament is not now nearly so dreadful as when the tyranny of coupons was at its height. Then it was in vain for a poor wretch to rush into a shop unless he had with him that odious pink clothing book full of brown and lilac tokens. The most charitable of Samaritan

146

vendors had to turn a deaf ear to his pleading. If he had suddenly found himself penniless he might have approached somebody of benevolent aspect, crying " O compassionate stranger, if you ever had a mother, lend me eighteen pence " or words to that effect. He would have been much more likely to be successful than if he had asked for the loan of a handkerchief. Thank goodness those worst days are over and there is for the forgetful a *locus poenitentiae*. We may hope that the Board of Trade's order applies only to utilitarian articles and not to those tending to improve the mind. Let it not touch those moral pocket handkerchiefs which, as Mr. Stiggins explained, " Combine amusement with instruction, blending select tales with woodcuts."

HENLEY

The very best and most effectual posture in a man is that of rowing, said an old writer, whose authority will not be questioned to-day, even by truants from Lord's or Wimbledon who have strayed to the Buckinghamshire or Berkshire bank of the Thames. Amateurs of less Spartan sports may shake their heads over the gruelling discipline to which oarsmen cheerfully submit. Watching a practice crew being bullied through the megaphone by a tyrant comfortably seated on a bicycle, even wicket-keepers thank the stars that they have escaped a galley slave's fate. Pity for " the eight poor souls whose meat is hard steak and a harder hen " might be tinged with envy, if an orgy of extra calories, however tough, were still the prerogative of the rowing men. Their meat ration having shrunk and the gallons of beer drunk at breakfast by their forerunners or, perhaps, forerowers, having been poured away down the sands of time, they have only, in the eyes of other sportsmen, the fun and glory of the race to sustain them.

At Henley it is enough. They come together from the ends of the earth and are seen with admiration, if not always with envy, by spectators whose clumsiness on the river would upset the heaviest old tub ever hired out by the hour. Henley has about it a flavour of history as well as of cosmopolitan charm. Cambridge had, it is true, won the Boat Race twice as often as Oxford, when the first Royal Regatta was held, and this might be said to lend the event a familiar, contemporary air ; but statistics are misleading and, on that far-off Friday in June, there had been only three university boat races. Rowing, like cricket, had not yet lost its free and easy manners and its uninhibited taste for dressing up. Gentlemen had to be forbidden to make the towpaths dangerous by furious horsemanship, and one college crew took the water resplendent in blue-striped guernseys, blue caps with gold tassels and rosettes of yellow, purple and crimson.

A hope was expressed by the promoters of that primeval Henley of the most beneficial results coming to themselves and to the public in general, if their enterprise was conducted "under judicious and respectable management." They would surely feel, were they to return now and be told of the close finishes, the dead heats, and the visitors from Japan westward round the world to Canada and the United States, that they had built better than they knew. Hundreds of foreign entries have reached Henley over the years. The fame of the Belgian Club Nautique de Grand will stand out in some memories, but only in a crowd which includes Swiss and Australians and still has a kindly place for that redoubtable Wiking Rudergesellschaft out of Nazi Germany. More than any other English setting, or so at least rowing men claim, Henley is the perfect spot for bringing together sportsmen from so many lands. It is almost a pleasure for hosts to be beaten, as they often are, when they can look round and ask where in the island or out of it athletes may compete in so pleasant a summer landscape. As the crews go out this week the staunchest believer in the decadence of modern rowing must be moved to admit

> Yet, still I think, he moves his blade,
> As grand in style or grander,
> As captain of some Happy-Shade
> Elysian Leander.

THINK, PUPPY, THINK

Lions and tigers, under the spell of nonchalant he-men and photogenic ladies of the circus, lie down like lambs. Learned pigs count up to ten and fleas can, somehow or other, be persuaded to qualify as performers. The way of the golden eagle has been by-passed into docile channels by masters of falconry, and there is no end to what can be done to educate a seal. Bears dance better than elderly gentlemen do in a night club, and horses learn gracefully to go through the intricate ceremonial devised at courts where etiquette was etiquette. Elephants allow Burmese urchins to shove them around and apparently like it. If African elephants show a less cooperative spirit and cats are about the hardest cases of all, these exceptions only rub in the rule that the most unlikely creatures prove, when wisely handled, apt scholars.

So it is humiliating that the aptest of the lot, the dog, grows up, nine times out of ten, into a dunce. This, as his owners know, is their fault. They lack the canine touch that, applied by a happy few, turns puppies into well-educated little gentlemen. " I have found it a great advantage," remarks one authority, " to get my dogs to stop immediately I say ' Stand.' " Who would not ? Who again (outside the charmed circle of those who have the equivalent of green fingers in a gardener) will not sigh on hearing the advice, just given, to begin on a puppy as soon as he is strong enough and *sensible enough* to absorb the " initial obedience work " ? The italics are not in the original, but they will be read into it by many a failed-trainer. Patience, a length of cord, and a pocketful of broken biscuits are all that is needed to drill a young dog in behaviour that would do credit to a guardsman Trooping the Colour. He will come to heel and

150

walk there, however zigzag a course his owner may follow. When he is told to sit down and stay put, he does so even if the instructor disappears round a corner. His master's voice—quiet, friendly, compelling—is his law. Every dog is a potential paragon. Give me the right teacher, he would say if he could talk, and I will finish the job.

How ashamed of his family circle he will subconsciously feel when, through lack of skilful guidance in youth, he finds himself fixing a magnetic eye on each mouthful that is eaten at the tea-table. Suppose some misguided sentimentalist throws him something? Where then is the healthy rule about only one good meal a day? His better nature overpowered by ill-discipline will incessantly be in agony. The better nature of terriers must lead a wretched life. They cannot be such little fools as their untrained behaviour suggests. If they were judged by that, they would be denied any sense of size and credited with a preposterous chivalry over sex. A placid but male Alsatian, under whose chassis they could run without bumping their heads, is flown at and murder in self-defence only averted by human aid. A mincing dachshund bitch sneaks their ball or curls up in their basket and they simper meekly. Their deafness when shouted at to come out of a covert is matched by an acute power of hearing when a door that may lead to a walk is opened. For every such backward pupil an incompetent owner is to blame. The culprit has one comfort. Dogs, it is said in informed circles, are never bored or low-spirited unless they live with bored, low-spirited people. Most owners, by this test, are evidently raging, tearing good company.

BOOLE ON ORDINARY DISCOURSE

We are often told that ignorance is bliss, and this may well be so ; but it very seldom feels like bliss. It is true that a deep, inner complacency, amounting in some cases to a form of glee, transfigures the faces of people who, when we ask them the way somewhere, reply that they do not know it and have indeed never heard of our alleged destination. But the young scholar who cannot name the capital of Tasmania, the guardsman who has to admit that the identity of his commanding officer is still a mystery to him, even the brazen politician obliged to reveal that he does not know how many tons of liquorice his department bought from Portuguese East Africa during 1949—these, as they make their confessions, exhibit few of the symptoms normally associated with ecstasy. They do not actually blub, or beat their breasts, or anything like that, but they look far from gruntled.

We have been trained—not without difficulty in the early stages—to regard knowledge as a precious commodity ; and although the fool, who has so little of it, is not nearly so greedy for more as the learned man, whose brain is simply bursting with the stuff, hardly anybody wishes to know less than he does. It is only rarely that the ordinary man can derive pleasure from not knowing something, but though—like so many of the ordinary man's other pleasures—this one is both base and transient, it does to some extent compensate him for all those other occasions when ignorance was so very far from blissful. When, for instance, he scans the examination papers which lately confronted the young ladies and gentlemen of Oxford University reading the Honour School of Philosophy, Politics, and Economics he is unlikely to be smitten with a sudden envious thirst for the Pierian spring. When he reads " Is $\Sigma p_2 q_2 > \Sigma p_2 q_1$ a satisfactory criterion of an increase in real national income ? " the fact that he does not know the answer does not fill him with a sense of shame ; he does not even particularly wish that he was able to pronounce the question. Nor is he conscious of an aching void in his education when he comes to " ' Statements made in ordinary discourse cannot be classified completely and exactly into logical types.' What would Boole's comment be ? " He does not know who Boole is—unless the examiners are referring to the T. L. K. Boole who was at a private school with him ; and even if they are (which seems on the whole unlikely) he has not seen this Boole for more than thirty years and has no idea at all what comment—if indeed any, for he was a rather silent little boy—he would have made on the statement quoted. It appears, at least it appears to anyone who has ever been to a cocktail party or even a regimental dinner, to be a statement of the obvious. But perhaps the Boole these examiners have in mind is a bit of a recluse and does not get about much in society. Perhaps he is the sort of silly fellow who believes that statements made in ordinary discourse can be classified completely and exactly into logical types. In that case his comment would probably be " Nonsense ! " or " I find myself unable to concur " or " Tell that to the Marines ! " It certainly does make it more difficult, not knowing what sort of a man Boole is. T. L. K. lived, as far as one can remember, in Tunbridge Wells, but this one may be an American. There is no means of knowing ; and one's consequent ignorance, though hardly to be described as bliss, seems a good deal less painful than it usually does.

CRUELTY TO PARENTS

The object of taking part in a race is to win it. Even in Great Britain, where we have developed in the course of centuries—providentially, as it now turns out—a certain aptitude for losing with a good grace, victory still remains the goal for which the athlete strives. He may only have half a chance, but he has a single mind. It is not perhaps quite the same with horses, whose motives often appear to be mixed and who sometimes—especially when we have hazarded on them some part of the moneys which we owe to the Inspector of Taxes—lose at a critical moment much of their interest in the proceedings. But by and large it remains true that the will to win animates all contestants in an athletic event, to the temporary exclusion of all other thoughts and emotions.

The suspension of this natural law is what lends an eerie fascination to the races for fathers and mothers organized at the school sports in which their progeny compete at this time of year. Although these trials of speed, like cock-fighting, badger-baiting, and the burning of witches, are relics of a more barbarous age, they have not yet been, like most other things, prohibited by legislation ; and doubtless our children, as they gather our great-grandchildren round their aged knees, will bore them stiff with inaccurate reminiscences of the unholy practices to which they once saw us obliged to lend ourselves. For it is, of course, obligatory for parents to enter, unless they are either very old indeed or have had the sense to hire a pair of crutches for the occasion.

The Mothers' Race is generally run first and—were it not for the doom hanging so imminently over their heads —their consorts might find something rather charming in the spectacle of these matrons—some lissom, some

154

not—legging it over the greensward, uttering (until their breath gives out) shrill and on the whole remarkable good-humoured cries. In only very few is the thought of victory uppermost. Some are worrying about their hats, others about their high heels, and all fear that beneath their fluttering draperies something will snap. Some skim, some thunder forward, determined not to disgrace themselves in the eyes of their children, and even more determined not to be beaten by any mother of obviously riper years. The winner's flanks are heaving as she rummages for a mirror in the handbag which her offspring (if male) has made furtive haste to return to her; but she feels agreeably youthful.

The Fathers' Race is a slightly more gruesome affair. No man wants to court a sudden death from heart failure and few wish to expose their braces to the public view; and the consciousness that they are all—quite unnecessarily —now doing both these things casts a certain gloom upon the fathers. The will to win burns strongly in a few, and many who cannot aspire to victory feel a stirring of the competitive spirit as they take station alongside their contemporaries. At last off they go, moving (it seems) with unparalleled velocity for the first twenty yards, then losing momentum and in the end finishing (if at all) the reverse of strongly. Their lungs are bursting, their vision is blurred, they find some difficulty in speaking. But at least they were not last, and they will not have to run a hundred yards again until next year. By that time, though their speed is most unlikely to have increased, they will with any luck have got a new pair of braces.

GAIETY, GOODBYE

The Gaiety has lain since before the war a sheer hulk
washed by the eddying tides of traffic that flow from
Fleet Street and Charing Cross and over Waterloo Bridge
and stagnate interminably where they meet. It is not old
as theatres go, for its namesake, made famous by
" PRACTICAL JOHN " HOLLINGSHEAD, gave way to the
present, doomed building early in the Edwardian era.
Even when GEORGE EDWARDES opened with EDMUND
PAYNE, GEORGE GROSSMITH and GERTIE MILLAR and
CONNIE EDISS in *The Orchid*, he was only continuing
along a theatrical path he had made familiar for nearly
twenty years. He was following the tradition of HOLLINGS-
HEAD, who, at the conversion of the Strand Music Hall
into the Gaiety of the sixties, said that the stage, whatever
it might be, " judged from the lofty not to say stuck-up
heights of literature and art," was not a platform for
the display of " grandmothers and maiden aunts."
EDWARDES thought the same (as others had done before
either of these managers of genius), but he did so with a
difference. The reign of the " Guvnor " reflected on
the Gaiety stage, more than light theatres always do,
something of the spirit of the times.

Burlesque under his guidance gave way to musical
comedy. Girl after girl, preceded by that pioneer charmer
who came from a " Shop," stepped out in front of the
rose-pink, green and gold setting, and some of them lived
to reach out for a tiara. " Molly, she married a marquis,"
if not the theme song of the shows (and from another
place), marked them off as sharply from Victorian
Coal Holes and Cider Cellars as it did from present-day
Hollywood. The Strand between Mafeking and Mons
looked to serious eyes such a silly when the moon shone

156

out, but the boy who bought tickets to see KATE CUTLER or LILY ELSIE and their attendant beauties guessed right every time. The " Guvnor " stuck to his girls and to those easily digested day-dreams that went down so well with audiences enlivened by champagne and groomed almost as exquisitely as the gentlemen of his chorus. More recent years kept up the fun, bringing in LESLIE HENSON and causing GRACIE FIELDS to be " chaired " as she left the stage door.

It would be foolish, in regretting that the Gaiety has ceased to be, to pitch excessive claims for its achievement. A little more cutting-edge to the wit, a dash of the satire and commentary on everyday affairs found in the better *revues* of the twenties and thirties would have added salt to the sometimes insipid performances of musical comedy in its prime. They were with their limitations an unambitious but a complete form of art. The present age would be more lively if it had a LIONEL MONCKTON and the rest. The importing of riotously tuneful athleticism is no substitute for a native school. GEORGE EDWARDES, although he never dug deep, was not a period figure to be forgotten as, to its shame, the *Dictionary of National Biography* has done. It is a pity that his old theatre cannot be towed down the Thames and sunk to a fusillade of popping corks. Clicking typewriters and the mutter of business letters being dictated will surely drown all echo of the laughter of the Gaiety girls.

PLAYING AT CRUSOE

The pairing of famous men to share, two and two like the animals in the ark, shipwreck on a raft might make a good round game, but no player is likely to suggest DISRAELI as an ideal opposite number for LEWIS CARROLL. Yet they would have had in their predicament at least one common antipathy to bring them together. " I never saw the use of the sea," wrote DISRAELI, and LEWIS CARROLL, going farther, sang " the thing I hate most is a thing they call the sea." They may have changed their minds, but on this evidence they are ruled out as owners of islands. The envy felt by many people for the lucky buyer on reading that Skomer off the coast of Pembrokeshire has been sold would not have afflicted them. Desire to own an island cannot be dismissed as a symptom of escapism. There is something more positive in it than that ; the challenge of having to look after oneself when cut off by storms is half the temptation ; hope that a man has resources enough in himself to be solitary without getting bored springs eternal.

How far experience would breed disillusion is another matter. Even MR. LOCKLEY, that most articulate and delightful of volunteer Robinson Crusoes, does not pretend that it is an easy life. Seen from the cliffs on a fine July evening with the sun going down behind them and lending them a halo of rosy light, islands do, indeed, beckon the walker on the mainland. Motorists, such is the power of an island spell, have been known to stop the cars, in which they were hurrying back to hot baths, cocktails and dancing, and get out to gaze and vow that there was nothing they would like better than to spend a winter, or at any rate an autumn, encircled by the sea and free from the cares of wheeled traffic. A wireless set, they boast at the vainglorious peak of their pipe dream, would be declared contraband. Bardsey divided by its treacherous tide race from Caernarvonshire, Sark and Alderney whispering invitation to trippers on Guernsey, the romantic outline of Crete viewed from the decks of a rolling liner—all call to travellers with the insidious salesmanship of the sirens on their island by Scylla and Charybdis.

From high cliffs and lonely beaches, broken against by the Atlantic waves, watchers peer longingly at the little sentinel bastions of dry land off Kerry and Connemara. Ushant is more than a landfall breaking the monotony of long days at sea. Thousands of passengers, passing and repassing it, have idly wished that they could add it to their bag of islands visited, but few Englishmen have set foot on its rugged shores. Sardinia and Corsica, seeming almost to join with tiny islets sprawling over the narrow straits of Bonifacio that so nearly do not separate them, appear, from an aircraft, to be delectable. The rude remarks of D. H. LAWRENCE are impossible to take seriously from that height. Sumatra looks full of mysterious possibilities as the flight is made beside it to Java, and British soldiers, homesick for their native island in the distant northern waters, still sometimes felt they could spare a few hours to explore it. To be out of sight is not, for an island, to be out of mind. Stornoway and all Lewis are often present, a *terra incognita* crying to be visited, in the thoughts of timid sailors who never venture beyond the harbour mouth of Ullapool. The ideal spot, unlike some of these, should be deserted, but to demand a desert island is going too far. Somewhere between that austere loneliness and discomfort sought for by the old hermits and the distracting amenities offered to beachcombers in Honolulu and Bermuda is the golden mean. Its latitude is within reach of three good meals a day and a waterproof cottage and well to the windward of the Chancellor of the Exchequer.

159

THE UTILITY OF FLEAS

Comparatively few of us really want to live in an ivory tower, especially if we are fond of elephants ; but we quite often find ourselves in moods or situations which automatically generate a craving for solitude. It may be that we wish to compose a poem, or to catch a fish, or to paint a landscape, or to rehearse the few well or anyhow very carefully chosen words with which we propose to open the village fête on Saturday ; we may want to watch a bird or to have a nap after luncheon ; we may even (though this is not very probable) want to think. If we lived in an ivory tower we should be, so to speak, on the mains as far as solitude is concerned ; it would be laid on. As it is, we often find it elusive. The problems of organizing a four at tennis or of recruiting an eleven for a cricket match are, though difficult, not insoluble. The problem of organizing a one at anything is infinitely less easy, and anybody who devised a formula which would meet this recurrent need would deserve the gratitude of mankind.

An Indian gentleman had a pretty good shot at it the other day, though he tackled the problem on a narrow and rather specialized front. What he discovered was the secret of how to get a railway compartment to oneself. Most of us, in our time, have made feeble, amateurish sorties at this desirable objective. We have tried pulling down the blinds ; we have leant, bulkily deterrent, out of the window, doing our best to look (in cases where this has been possible) more like a homicidal maniac than we do already ; we have burst into paroxysms of sepulchral coughing as an intruder appeared at the door. It has never really worked. As often as not we have ended our journey with two dear little children romping stickily on the seat beside us while their mother and their aunt exchange interminable details of the ailments to which the other members of the family have lately fallen victim.

The Indian gentleman would have got rid of these in no time. His technique—for, though it was only accidentally tested on the Orient express the other day, he will surely revert to it deliberately when the need arises— his technique is based on a box containing 300 performing fleas. When this fell from the luggage rack and burst open he soon found himself, although the train was crowded, alone save for his talented troupe. This trifling mishap will surely not be the last of its kind, though it may easily be the most fortuitous. Few living creatures are easier to transport on the hoof than fleas, and henceforth no enterprising traveller will fail to provide himself with a few hundred of them in a suitable receptacle. They may not, it is true, be performing fleas in the generally accepted sense of the word ; but after all they will be required to take part in only one quite simple trick, and they ought to manage that all right.

THE GOOD EARTH

It is the time of year when the free countryman exiled in London is obliged to temper his customary disdain for the disciplined nature that he sees about him with a little appreciation of high summer in the city. Forgetting the scathing eloquence he has in the past poured on the spectacle of off-white sheep grazing among deck-chairs, and unnaturally docile water-fowl ignobly competing with clockwork boats, he, reared among the stern and wild, eyes with favour gay window-boxes bursting with geraniums and nasturtiums, the pink mist of willow herb on bombed sites, and mellow wallflowers glowing in ancient sunlight on Gothic parapets. More than that, he buys seeds, cadges cuttings, pleads for plants and bespeaks boxes from his grocer. There remains the earth : now earth is indispensable, whether for the nurture of gloxinias, yuccas or crops that are normally admitted only through the back door ; but earth, the raw material, is hard to come by in the city. On making inquiries, the shocked countryman is told by window-boxers that soil can be bought. To one brought up among masses of the stuff this is a staggering blow. While he has been willing to defend his native earth against a common enemy, the idea of buying with sterling about a breadbinful is repellent.

Nor do the alternatives suggested by friends seem any more attractive ; a visit to a market stall at the end of the day, culling, as it were, crumbs from the rich man's table, does not recommend itself any more than a mission to the glades of St. John's Wood or a trek to the foothills of Hampstead. It is a sad business, reflects the exile, eyeing thoughtfully a cluster of Cupids sulkily supporting a stone bowl of flagging begonias ; with difficulty he dismisses the base thought that comes to his mind. How could his tomato plants flourish in soil obtained in such an unethical manner ? Eventually, fate in the guise of a kindly builder's foreman, wooed over light ale, and discoursing of earth in terms of cubic yards, resolves the problem by granting digging rights on the site of a block of flats in course of erection. To transport the good earth through a mile of London streets is a weighty matter, for if there is a more arduous task than moving Heaven it is moving earth, and never more so than when moving it in a cycle basket insulated with an old newspaper. Trundling along with his prize the man on the bicycle wonders if the city fathers could not release from their stocks earth for all. Birds have baths ; dogs, little dishes of china ; horses, fountains ; and children, sandpits ; why should he and his like not find neat dumps of soil in public places ? But this he knows to be vain dreaming.

M

FILMING TOM BROWN

Now that the school term is ending it is possible tranquilly to digest the thought of Tom Brown being filmed against his authentic background at Rugby and with the help of the Board of Governors. It will be received by many people at once with a pleasurable excitement and a certain jealous apprehension. These sentiments are, indeed, inseparable from the dramatization, whether on the stage or on the screen, of any much-loved book, but *Tom Brown's School Days* is peculiarly calculated to arouse them. Not only is it a very great, if occasionally irritating book, but it is one lending itself to exact, perhaps irritatingly exact, quotation, tainted with exhibitionism. It has not a few devotees, by no means all of them Rugbeians, each of whom is arrogantly prepared to put down his money and back himself against all comers in a Tom Brown match, as to the name of the horse that Tom drew in the Derby lottery or of the hero that held his own against the Cock of the Louts. One of the first scenes to be filmed—work on which was begun yesterday—is that of a game of Rugby football as it was played not long after the days of WILLIAM WEBB ELLIS. That should be intensely interesting and will, for the uninitiated, throw some light on the rather mysterious proceedings between the scoring of the try by Young Brooke and the kicking of the goal by Old Brooke.

Incidentally, the faithful may wonder what will be done about the celebrated Three Trees, which are now no more. Unless memory shamefully errs, Old Brooke gave the order to play strongly for touch by the Three Trees and his brother's try directly ensued from that manoeuvre. Can the skill of the producer produce even dummy trees or must we do without them ? The question is doubtless both pedantic and absurd and yet the reverent, un-Rugbeian mind longs to know. It is interesting to observe that the distinguished actors who a short while since were respectively a ferocious Bill Sikes and pathetic Oliver Twist are now to be translated into Dr. Arnold and Tom Brown. Tom will have to sprout rather rapidly, it would seem, if he is to end as Captain of the Eleven, nineteen years old, but great are the wonders of production. It is to be feared that certain foreign observers may once again be inclined to take us and our books too literally. A little while ago they declared that we conducted our General Election on Eatanswill principles. Now they will doubtless assert that the roasting of small boys is an everyday practice giving rise to general jollity and that Flashman—he always had more pocket-money than other people—was typical of the capitalist classes. However, that risk must be run and is well worth the running.

BY ANY OTHER NAME

A short while ago, a hotel in the south of England, missing from the mantelpiece in the lounge a champagne jeroboam, appealed through a small newspaper advertisement to whomsoever had removed the bottle—though so fine a vessel as a jeroboam can scarcely be designated a bottle—for its return. Bearing in mind the acquisitive instinct latent in all of us, the drafter of the notice can hardly have been sanguine that it would be restored. But he must have known his man, for at the end was the *cri du coeur* : " Its loss has spoilt an interesting set of bottles." Here, surely, was deep calling unto deep, for within a fortnight the return of the jeroboam was publicly acknowledged and the anonymous sender thanked for his, or her, prompt response to the appeal.

Into this story, apologue is not too strong a word, might be read proof of the high ethics of the real collector, the lofty plane on which the practitioners of barter and swap conduct their affairs. Nevertheless, it begs the question : " When is a collector not a collector ? " There can be no clouded view of the place of the seeded collector, recognized and admired, who assembles with enormous zeal the shells of birds' eggs, undevalued coinage, autographs, postage stamps, and unusably fragile china. His transactions and erudite research not seldom contribute to the sum total of human knowledge, and his conventions, conferences and rallies—though the term is a thought bucolic—are reported with care and respect in the specialist Press. To him is imputed no suggestion of mercenary gain, though he would be the first to deny that not infrequently his property represents a tidy sum. Indeed, there may yet come a time when the perplexed investor, sickened of nugatory returns from his stocks, may decide to risk his shirt on an Undemokratian 5 millenium crimson, depicting the People's Choice unveiling a new purge ; an issue quickly withdrawn and thus made rare, with a curious overprint : " Let Right Prevail."

The place of those who assemble match-box tops, bus tickets, orange wrappers, beer mats, and motor-car catalogues is, perhaps, not quite as sure, but certainly they are accorded a warm feeling not extended to the rank deviationists who acquire, through uncommercial channels, wash-basin plugs, electric bulbs from buses, colour prints from railway carriages and hotel towels. No doubt all are one when it comes to the appraisal of their trophies. The wildfowler, eyeing the drake smew in its glass mausoleum, recalls the bitter glory of the January day when it fell to his gun ; the china collector gazing through the glass door of his cabinet, the small shop in Ross-on-Wye where he nailed that Rockingham jug ; and the autograph hunter, flicking through the pages of his album, the stirring siege of the Palladium where he secured the signature of a transatlantic vocalist. The joys of the chase are not confined to the purely physical pursuits.

I SHALL NEVER FORGET

The older we grow, the greater becomes the probability that we shall from time to time meet friends or acquaintances whom we have not seen for a number of years. The pleasure which we derive from these encounters is sometimes very great, but it cannot be denied that they are fraught with problems of a peculiarly delicate kind. Few of us have not been puzzled and even disturbed by the contrast between the ease with which other people recognize us and the extraordinary difficulty which we find in identifying them. The cry " By Jove, if it isn't old Smith ! " ought to arouse in the individual to whom it is addressed—provided, of course, that his name is Smith—none save agreeable emotions. The face of the rather elderly man who has uttered this cry is suffused with *bonhomie*. But to whom does that face belong? At what stage of his career did Smith win the affection and esteem of its owner? Were they once neighbours? Or classmates? Or fellow-passengers or comrades-in-arms or rivals in love or what? Smith cannot for the life of him remember.

The nature of the tie that binds them will almost inevitably reveal itself, however, and Smith will soon know whether he last heard this voice from the past on Upper Sixpenny or on the promenade deck, at Benghazi or at Bari or at Barrackpore. The man's face will rearrange itself, losing (or perhaps adding) a moustache, restoring the dilapidations which time, the great healer, has effected, and reshuffling itself into a collection of features which were once—though not under a bowler hat—familiar. But what on earth is the fellow's name? By the time Smith realizes that he will never come any nearer to remembering it than a vague suspicion that it may have

168

begun with a G he has got back on to such cordial, *tutoyant* terms with the un- (or anyhow imperfectly) known that it is far too late to admit that the fellow's name has somehow failed to get itself enshrined in his memory. It is with a feeling of guilty hypocrisy that he writes down, on parting, a telephone number which he knows he can never use.

Perhaps the most awkward of all the awkward developments to which these reunions can lead is when we are credited by our long-lost friend with a part in some incident with which, though for all we know it may have taken place, we are perfectly certain that we had nothing to do. " I shall never forget," he begins ; or perhaps " The thing I shall always remember about you was ————." And then follows a detailed but as far as we are concerned wholly apocryphal description of some exploit or escapade in which we are supposed to have taken part. It may, indeed it generally does, exhibit us in a favourable light and it would not injure our credit at all to say with a modest laugh, " Fancy you remembering that silly business ! " and let it go at that. But our past, however inglorious, is our own and though his gloss may enliven the dull story of our life we greatly prefer our own version ; while the fact that we live in his memory on the strength of somebody else's achievements hurts our vanity. Yet he has said that he will never forget this thing, that it is what he will always remember us by. It seems a little hard to disabuse him. So when he asks (as he almost inevitably does) " And by the way, did you ever get your trousers back from the Proctor ? " or " What became of the Brigadier's jeep in the end ? " we can seldom quite bring ourselves to destroy the curious little myth. Instead we mutter, shuffling, that we cannot remember now, it all happened such a long time ago. It is society's fault, not ours, if a lack of candour is often a social virtue.

"THROWN OUT"

A correspondent asked the other day for some recognition in the score-book for the fielder who throws the wicket down; his plea will command the sympathy of all those who feel that fielding remains the most neglected branch of the game. He would have the score-card of the last Test match read not " Simpson, run out, 94," a vague and colourless description, but " Simpson, thrown out Rae, 94," which is altogether more vivid and dramatic. Once the principle is granted, however, all kinds of difficulties arise. Even supposing our correspondent is right, and that RAE did actually hit the stumps and not return the ball, according to the best text-book traditions, straight into the wicketkeeper's hands an inch or two above the bails, is not that throw just as meritorious as one that actually hits the stumps? And how can the difference be made clear between an underhand lob from a few yards away, when both batsmen are in the middle of the pitch confused in calls, mind and objective, and the inspired pounce and " throw out " from cover point in the tradition of VERNON ROYLE, G. L. JESSOP and HOBBS?

Fielding, it is true, is not " written up " as batting and bowling are; it lacks, as it were, the services of a publicity agent and is apt to be neglected by those who choose England XIs on the backs of envelopes. Fielding may be the Cinderella of the game, going busily about her work while her more flamboyant sisters flaunt their hundreds and their hat-tricks; when she does go to the ball, however, there is none can hold a candle to her. CLEMENT HILL played many great innings in his life, but never can he have experienced such joy as when he made that catch in the deep off a drive of LILLEY'S with perhaps the greatest of all Test matches in the balance, and what

6 A. P. F. CHAPMAN ever hit could compare with the thrill of his discovery that he had stretched out a miraculous hand and caught WOODFULL when the thing seemed a plain and palpable impossibility? Nothing of all this can be set down in detail on the score-card, and a pity it is, but there is a reverse side to the argument—there are things that fielders do for which they must bless the anonymity that normally cloaks their actions. The newest score-boards appear to have devices by which electric bulbs betray the identity of the individual fieldsman, cruel publicity for short-leg who has just dropped a sitter, but not even the most glaring neon light could be as terrible as the threat once uttered by the wisest and most Olympian of cricket correspondents to a famous player who had shown signs of slackness in the field. " If he offends again," ran in effect the dread decree, " he shall be named." Better to leave things as they are ; the good fieldsman, even if nobody has a kind word for him, goes in to bat happy in the knowledge that he cannot score a duck—twenty-five or so invisible runs are already under his number on the score-board.

THE HEIGHT OF REALISM

The news that the citizens of Canterbury are being asked to grow beards has been received calmly in Kent, and in the less adjacent parts of our archipelago has evoked that stoical resolve to carry on as usual which is often mistaken, by the more sensible type of foreigner, for apathy or indifference. Yet this request—which one rather supposes to be addressed, primarily at any rate, to the male inhabitants—is by no means a frivolous one. Nor is there any reason to postulate the existence, in this fine old town, of a deep-laid conspiracy against its barbers.

It is, rather, in aid of the Festival of Britain that these growths are to be cultivated. Canterbury intends to recall the glories of her past in a big way, and the pageants and other mummeries involved call for a large and unusually hirsute cast. No fair-minded person would feel justified in criticizing our ancestors for shaving as little as they did ; but there is no doubt that their habits in this respect do from time to time complicate matters for their descendants. Wigs are bad enough, but false beards are the very devil. It is one thing to hook over one's ears the sort of degenerate sporran which, in the uncertain light of candles on the Christmas tree, throws Santa Claus's less sophisticated beneficiaries into paroxysms of terror. It is quite another to cause, with the aid of spirit-gum, false hair to adhere to one's jowls in such a way that it will not fall off when one has to shout " Long live Queen Bess ! " or " Forward to Nottingham ! " or to make one's contribution to what the stage directions generally call " a deep-throated roar of approval."

Nor is maintenance of the *status quo* the sole function of a false beard. He who dons one—even if in the programme he figures only among the " Jutes, Legionaries, Burghers, Men-at-Arms, Friars, Courtiers, Knights, French Prisoners, Moors, Peasants, Smugglers, Air Raid Wardens, Citizens of the Future, &c."—must nevertheless be recognizable as a human being. Nothing more surely or more dangerously distracts the attention of an audience from a scene dealing (say) with the Wars of the Roses than a growing suspicion that one of the obscurer parti- cipants is intended to represent the Monster of Glamis ; and an impression of this kind is all too easily generated when an amateur cast with a long tail starts putting on false beards. As for taking them off again, this is a process which, among the unskilled, really demands a local anaesthetic ; and on humanitarian as well as on artistic and economic grounds, the Canterbury Festival Committee are to be congratulated on their far-sighted and imagina- tive project. The only thing to be said against it is that it will detract from the only unalloyed pleasure of dressing up, which lies in suddenly seeing how absolutely ridiculous one's friends look in their strange disguises. But, after all, beards in their formative phases are curious and sometimes risible phenomena ; so as far as Canterbury is concerned this pleasure can perhaps be described as not lost, but gone before.

THE QUIET WAY

The painstaking reader of the news will have noticed with some surprise, in these tight times, the emergence of a factor called redundancy. He had not been conscious, either in his own affairs or in the state of the nations, of any great super-abundance or superfluity of anything, save perhaps of tumult and tribulation. He had not felt himself to be " abounding to excess," nor observed in the fortunes of his friends and countrymen a lot of " swelling up and overflowing." Nor, in fact, had the economists, who are not thinking of our money when they use this noun of plenty, but of labouring men who here and there are " surplus to requirements." There is no brutal unemployment now, but only this " redundancy," which sounds just as important and is clearly a matter of plenitude, not of want. It simply needs explaining to the redundant themselves and to all the prospective redundant. The witness who confessed the other day that he " keeps very quiet at the office for fear they might think me redundant " seems not to have grasped how kind is the fate that threatens him.

Hearts will go out to this poor fellow, not only because of his very human fears, but because he seems so innocently to have overlooked the road to success in life. How can he have failed to notice the ways of those who win the race, or at any rate appear to lead in it ? How swiftly they stride about the office, dispatches in hand ; how fearlessly they face the chief ; how tall they tower above the typewriters and telephones and timid men. How dashing are their signatures, how firm their tread, how loud and clear their voices. Someone ought to tell that shy, retiring witness that keeping very quiet in his corner

174

is the very last thing he ought to do. He might retort, of course, that getting on is not his aim, but simply staying in. And it may be that, quietly stone-walling, he will keep his end up when all about him wickets fall. One hopes, indeed, that it will be so. The aim is harmless if not heroic, and " the best of men have ever loved repose."

RING A RING O' ROSES

Life for a starfish, said a recent broadcaster, is not a
bed of roses. Being a kindly man, anxious to avoid
depressing his listeners, he hastened to add that there
are compensations for a starfish and triumphs of survival
unattainable by the fittest of mortal men. If, for instance,
a crab bites off and eats four of its arms it can live to grow
four new ones, and if it eats something poisonous itself it
can match that mythical nursery trick of throwing out
the baby with the bath water. Poison and stomach
containing it are together ejected and no harm done. All
this is very nice for the starfish, but some listeners,
emotionally allergic to the joys and sorrows of the rock
pool, must have found their thoughts straying into deeper
waters. For whom is life—for whom has life ever been—
a bed of roses ?

The bed of Procrustes may seem, to-day, to provide
a nearer parallel. That hospitable Greek had, it will be
remembered, two beds, a short one into which he put
his tall visitors, after lopping off their superfluous inches,
and a long one, where the little chaps, having been
lengthened out to match, reposed. Resting uneasily on
the twin beds of cost of living that calls for a longer and
longer income and rate of taxation that leaves the income
shorter and shorter, the heir of all the ages, including
two world wars and a turbulent interlude of peace, feels
that never have so many had to put up with so much.
The Russians are too well equipped with good tanks and
the West Indians with good cricketers. There is seldom
a seat in the train in the morning and a new suit costs as
much as SIR CHARLES COCHRAN spent in happier days on
dressing his star gentleman to appear with credit through
a whole evening of regardless-of-expense revue. The time

176

is out of joint and the cursed spite of it is that wise and well-meaning men, like PRESIDENT TRUMAN, Mr. ATTLEE, MR. CHURCHILL, and the listener himself, inattentive to the tale of the starfish, are not given the free hand they deserve in setting it all right. That causes for self-pity exist to-day and are beyond the control of the sufferer is only too plain. What is overlooked is that in ages in which there seems, glancing back, every reason for general self-satisfaction, people found it necessary to invent excuses for pessimism.

METTERNICH, gloomily surveying the early part of the nineteenth century into which fate had pitched him, wished that he had been born in 1900. He lived to be eighty-six, and so, had he been granted his desire, he would now have the first half of the twentieth century behind him and another thirty and more years of it to face. It is a beautiful thought of so vintage a reactionary figure. This is the classic example of a man discontented with his own time, but it is a common kind of escapism, encountered even in apparently halcyon periods of history. Urge to bolt from the present into the past or future is matched by a singular capacity, noticeable in every generation, for nosing out contemporary enemies of mental peace and quiet. GOSSE told how his father, finding the servants indulging in Christmas pudding on the appropriate feast day—of which he disapproved—bore off to the dustbin the " idolatrous confectionery." Such a storm in the teacup of bigotry is laughable only to those who lack imaginative sympathy with their ancestors. This mutiny in his kitchen upset GOSSE *père*, one may be sure, as much as, had he been alive to-day, he would have been distressed by the invasion of Korea. There is no rhyme or reason in the things that men discover to worry about. There has never been a bed of roses free from thorns. A lesson might after all be learned from the starfish as useful as the one BRUCE got from his spider.

177